THREE·WAY MIRROR

2 FICTION : / NON-FICTION

PILOT ENGL. 10

© Nelson Canada,
A Division of International Thomson Limited, 1989

All rights in this book are reserved.

Published in 1989 by
Nelson Canada,
A Division of International Thomson Limited
1120 Birchmount Road
Scarborough, Ontario M1K 5G4

ISBN 0-17-603093-X
Teacher's Guide ISBN 0-17-603094-8

In-house Editor: Linda Bishop
Design: Rob McPhail
Cover Illustration: Sandra Dionisi

Printed and bound in Canada
by John Deyell Company

1234567890/JD/8765432109

Canadian Cataloguing in Publication Data

Main entry under title:

Three-way mirror

ISBN 0-17-603093-X

1. Short stories, Canadian (English) - 20th
century.* 2. Canadian literature (English) - 20th
century.* 3. Short stories, English - 20th century.
4. English literature - 20th century. 5. Readers
(Secondary). I. MacNeill, James A., 1933-   .

PS8321.T48 1989   C813'.01'08   C89-093803-2
PR9197.2.T48 1989

THREE•WAY MIRROR

REFLECTIONS IN FICTION AND NON•FICTION

Edited by James A. MacNeill

Nelson Canada

C O N T E N T S

What does being a winner mean? Being number one?

Beating the odds? Or just feeling good about yourself?

This unit looks at three very different people with

very different goals. What makes them winners?

RICK HANSEN:
MAN IN MOTION

Richard Scrimger

O n May 22, 1987, thousands of people lined the streets of Vancouver to watch, to cheer, and to bear witness as Rick Hansen completed his *Man in Motion* tour around the world. It was 2:00 p.m. local time when he rolled through a throng of reporters and dignitaries into the Oakridge Centre—the place where he'd begun his quest more than two years and forty thousand kilometres earlier.

"Actually," Hansen said, "the whole idea for the tour began way back in 1973." That was the year when fifteen-year-old Hansen was thrown from the back of a pick-up truck on his way home from a fishing trip. His back was broken in the accident, his spinal cord cut in two. The doctors said he would never walk again.

Hansen, an all-star athlete in basketball, volleyball, and track and field, decided that his disability was not going to stop him from competing. He joined a team of wheelchair athletes in his native British Columbia, practising and competing with them while at the same time going to school. (One of Hansen's teammates, and a good friend, was a young man who had just lost a leg to cancer. His name was Terry Fox.) By the time Hansen graduated from the University of British Columbia with a degree in Physical Education, he and his teammates were national champions in wheelchair basketball and volleyball.

For Hansen, being a university graduate and champion athlete failed to distract him from yet another goal: to conduct a long-distance wheelchair tour. He knew, however, that to accomplish such a goal would take a great deal of preparation. He continued to work on his strength and endurance and to compete in athletic events. Over the next four years, he won nineteen wheelchair marathons, including the 1983 Boston Marathon. In the 1982 Pan American Wheelchair Games in Halifax, Hansen won nine gold medals for Canada. Also in 1982, he shared the Lou Marsh Trophy as the top Canadian athlete with Wayne Gretzky. In 1984, Hansen won a gold and two silver medals at the World Wheelchair Games in England. The list of Hansen's athletic accomplishments grew and grew.

Finally, Hansen was ready to start planning his long journey. The next months were busy ones: picking the route, making arrangements to travel across the Atlantic and Pacific oceans, writing and telephoning ahead to publicize the tour, and trying to get pledges of support from governments, corporations, and the public. Hansen's goal was to raise $10 000 000 for spinal cord research. He did not have a large, organized team with him; he and a few friends made all the preparations themselves.

March 21, 1985, was wet and grey in Vancouver. The roads were slippery. After shaking hands with the mayor, Rick Hansen headed south. A few hundred people in the Oakridge Centre applauded; most went on with their shopping. Television cameras followed Hansen and the motor home where he would sleep. On its first turn out of the centre, the motor home crashed into a low overpass, damaging its roof and a spare wheelchair. The *Man in Motion* tour was under way.

A few days later, Hansen's shoulder was hurting badly and he had developed tendonitis in both wrists. He was only in Oregon.

The tour seemed to be ending before it had really begun. "That was one low point," Hansen said later. "I thought: 'I don't believe this; I've still got two years to go!'"

There would be other low points. At the start, the tour got little publicity and even less financial support. Hansen's fund grew very slowly as he rolled south toward Texas. In England, in the summer, he was ill with the flu; in France, a leak in the motor home gave him carbon monoxide poisoning; in the Alps, his tendonitis and shoulder pain flared up again; and in Portugal he was struck with a virus. Still, Hansen carried on, wheeling a daily average of eighty kilometres, uphill and down, through fair weather and foul. In Greece, in December, Hansen collapsed twice from the accumulated strain, but he refused to give up the tour or even to rest for long. Before the end of the month he was on the road again, tucked into his familiar hunch, his torso bent forward over his legs, his powerful arms and shoulders pulling in a steady rhythm.

The trip was not all hardship, of course. There were good moments, many of them, along the way. Like the time the soldiers on both sides of the Israeli-Jordanian border pulled away, saluting, to allow him to pass. Or the Chinese government giving him permission to travel along the Great Wall. Or the weeks in Australia and New Zealand spent relaxing on the smooth, white beaches, soaking in the warmth of summer. Or his arrival in Newfoundland in August, 1986. "It felt good," Hansen said. "Good to be home. Even though there was still a long way to go."

A long way is right. Hansen had wheeled through thirty-four countries and as many thousand kilometres, but he had only raised $200 000. Now he had six thousand or so kilometres of the Trans-Canada Highway ahead of him, and most of the money still to find. He was dead tired after a year and a half of daily grind, his arm and back and shoulders weary—and he was where Terry Fox and Steve Fonyo had been when they started.

By now, though, Hansen had captured the country's attention. The media began to follow him closely; his stops along the way to talk and to raise money became more frequent and more successful. In what Hansen was doing, and in what he was saying, the real purpose of the tour clearly emerged. Here was a young man overcoming a disability and, in doing so, accomplishing an incredible athletic feat. "The real tragedy," Hansen said of the tour, "would be if everyone gave a dollar and then forgot all about the disabled."

Hansen made sure that the country did not forget about him or his cause. On October 26, on Parliament Hill in Ottawa, he met the Prime Minister and received a government cheque for $1 000 000. A week later, 6000 people crowded Nathan Philips Square in Toronto to hear him speak. Thousands more lined the streets to watch and applaud. By the time he reached Saskatchewan, Hansen had raised $6 000 000, and the fund was growing every day.

He was still in pain. His shoulders had never really healed; his overworked muscles ached with every pull. His support team worked harder than ever for him but, as he wrote at mid-tour, "Sometimes you know you are the only person out there and no one can feel what you are feeling."

One unexpected bonus was the weather. Hansen had expected to meet bitter cold and harsh, driving snow, but the winter of 1986-87 was the mildest the Prairies had seen in years. He pushed himself onward, increasing the pace, taking advantage of the good weather while it lasted.

His grim determination did not abate until he was over the Rockies; then, with this last mountain range behind him, wheeling homeward down the Fraser River Valley, Hansen let himself show some relief, some joy.

It was on May 22, in the middle of Vancouver springtime, that the *Man in Motion* tour ended. Rick Hansen had raised more than $10 000 000 and had focused world attention on the efforts of the disabled. The thousands who watched him in person, and the millions who watched him on television, saw an athlete of strength and determination who happened to be disabled—not a handicapped person who happened to be strong. As one speaker said, commemorating the end of the tour, "Rick Hansen has changed the way we see ourselves. More important, he has changed the way we see each other."

Rick Hansen is an athlete and a hero to people of all abilities. He speaks not just for himself and other athletes, but for all of us when he says, "The point is, we do our best because we all face obstacles, and it's how we deal with them that determines the success or failure of our lives."

RAYMOND'S RUN

T o n i   C a d e   B a m b a r a

I don't have much work to do around the house like some girls. My mother does that. And I don't have to earn my pocket money by working; George runs errands for the big boys and sells Christmas cards. And anything else that's got to get done, my father does. All I have to do in life is mind my brother Raymond, which is enough.

Sometimes I slip and say my little brother Raymond. But as any fool can see he's much bigger and he's older too. But a lot of people call him my little brother 'cause he needs looking after 'cause he's not quite right. And a lot of smart mouths got lots to say about that too, especially when George was minding him. But now, if anybody has anything to say to Raymond, anything to say about his big head, they have to come by me. And I don't play the dozens or believe in standing around with somebody in my face doing a lot of talking. I'd much rather just knock you down and take my chances even if I am a little girl with skinny arms and a squeaky voice, which is how I got the name Squeaky. And if things get too rough, I run. And as anybody can tell you, I'm the fastest thing on two feet.

There is no track meet that I don't win the first place medal. I used to win the twenty-metre dash when I was a little kid in kindergarten. Nowadays, it's the fifty-metre dash. And tomorrow

I'm subject to run the quarter-kilometre relay all by myself and come in first, second, and third. The big kids call me Mercury 'cause I'm the swiftest thing in the neighbourhood. Everybody knows that—except two people who know better, my father and me. He can beat me to Amsterdam Avenue with me having a two fire-hydrant head start and him running with his hands in his pockets and whistling. But that's private information. 'Cause can you imagine some thirty-five-year-old man stuffing himself into shorts to race little kids? So as far as everyone's concerned, I'm the fastest and that goes for Gretchen, too, who has put out the tale that she is going to win the first-place medal this year. Ridiculous. In the second place, she's got short legs. In the third place, she's got freckles. In the first place, no one can beat me and that's all there is to it.

I'm standing on the corner admiring the weather and about to take a stroll down Broadway so I can practise my breathing exercises, and I've got Raymond walking on the inside close to the buildings, 'cause he's subject to fits of fantasy and starts thinking he's a circus performer and that the curb is a tightrope strung high in the air. And sometimes after a rain he likes to step down off his tightrope right into the gutter and slosh around getting his shoes and cuffs wet. Then I get it when I get home. Or sometimes if you don't watch him he'll dash across the traffic to the island in the middle of Broadway and give the pigeons a fit. Then I have to go behind him apologizing to all the old people sitting around trying to get some sun and getting all upset with the pigeons fluttering around them, scattering their newspapers and upsetting the wax-paper lunches in their laps. So I keep Raymond on the inside of me, and he plays like he's driving a stage coach which is O.K. by me so long as he doesn't run me over or interrupt my breathing exercises, which I have to do on account of I'm serious about my running and I don't care who knows it.

Now some people like to act like things come easy to them, won't let on that they practise. Not me. I'll high-prance down 34th Street like a rodeo pony to keep my knees strong even if it does get my mother uptight so that she walks ahead like she's not with me, doesn't know me, is all by herself on a shopping trip, and I am somebody else's crazy child. Now you take Cynthia Procter for instance. She's just the opposite. If there's a test tomorrow, she'll say something like, "Oh, I guess I'll play hand-ball this afternoon and watch television tonight," just to let you know she isn't thinking about the test. Or like last week when she won the spelling bee for the millionth time, "A good thing you got 'receive,' Squeaky, 'cause I would have got it wrong. I completely forgot about the spelling bee." And she'll clutch the lace on her blouse like it was a narrow escape. Oh, brother. But of course when I pass her house on my early morning trots around the block, she is practising the scales on the piano over and over and over and over. Then in music class she always lets herself get bumped around so she falls accidently on purpose onto the piano stool and is so surprised to find herself sitting there that she decides just for fun to try out the ole keys. And what do you know—Chopin's waltzes just spring out of her fingertips and she's the most surprised thing in the world. A regular prodigy. I could kill people like that. I stay up all night studying the words for the spelling bee. And you can see me any time of the day practising running. I never walk if I can trot, and shame on Raymond if he can't keep up. But of course he does, 'cause if he hangs back someone's likely to walk up to him and get smart, or take his allowance from him, or ask him where he got that great big pumpkin head. People are so stupid sometimes.

So I'm strolling down Broadway breathing out and breath-ing in on counts of seven, which is my lucky number, and here comes Gretchen and her side-kicks: Mary Louise, who used to be a friend of mine when she first moved to Harlem from Baltimore and got beat up by everybody 'till I took up for her on account of her mother and my mother used to sing in the same choir when they were young girls, but people aren't grateful, so now she hangs out with the new girl, Gretchen, and talks about me like a dog; and Rosie, who is as fat as I am skinny and has a big mouth where Raymond is concerned and is too stupid to know that there is not a big deal of difference between herself and Raymond and that she can't afford to throw stones. So they are steady coming up Broadway and I see right away that it's going to be one of those Dodge City scenes 'cause the street isn't that big and they're close to the buildings just as we are. First I think I'll step into the candy store and look over the new comics and let them pass. But that's chicken and I've got a reputation to consider. So then I think I'll just walk straight on through them or even over them if necessary. But as they get to me, they slow down. I'm ready to fight, 'cause like I said I don't feature a whole lot of chit-chat, I much prefer to just knock you down right from the jump and save everybody a lotta precious time.

"You signing up for the May Day races?" smiled Mary Louise, only it's not a smile at all. A dumb question like that doesn't deserve an answer. Besides, there's just me and Gretchen standing there really, so no use wasting my breath talking to shadows.

"I don't think you're going to win this time," says Rosie, trying to signify with her hands on her hips all salty, completely forgetting that I have whupped her behind many times for less salt than that.

"I always win 'cause I'm the best," I say straight at Gretchen who is, as far as I'm concerned, the only one talking in this ventriloquist-dummy routine. Gretchen smiles, but it's not a smile, and I'm thinking that girls never really smile at each other because they don't know how and don't want to know how and there's probably no one to teach us how, 'cause grown-up girls don't know either. Then they all look at Raymond who has just brought his mule team to a standstill. And they're about to see what trouble they can get into through him.

"What grade you in now, Raymond?"

"You got anything to say to my brother, you say it to me, Mary Louise Williams of Raggedy Town, Baltimore."

"What are you, his mother?" sasses Rosie.

"That's right, Fatso. And the next word out of anybody and I'll be *their* mother too." So they just stand there and Gretchen shifts from one leg to the other and so do they. Then Gretchen puts her hands on her hips and is about to say something with her freckle-face self but doesn't. Then she walks around me looking me up and down but keeps walking up Broadway, and her side-kicks follow her. So me and Raymond smile at each other and he says "Gidyap" to his team and I continue with my breathing exercises, strolling down Broadway toward the ice man on 145th with not a care in the world 'cause I am Miss Quicksilver herself.

I take my time getting to the park on May Day because the track meet is the last thing on the program. The biggest thing on the program is the May Pole dancing, which I can do without, thank you, even if my mother thinks it's a shame I don't take part and "act like a girl for a change." You'd think my mother'd be grateful not to have to make me a white organdy dress with a big satin sash and buy me new white baby-doll shoes that can't be taken out of the box 'till the big day. You'd think she'd be glad her daughter isn't out there prancing around a May Pole getting the new clothes all dirty and sweaty and trying to act like a flower or whatever you're supposed to be when you should be trying to be yourself, whatever that is, which is, as far as I am concerned, a poor black girl who really can't afford to buy shoes and a new dress you only wear once a lifetime 'cause it won't fit next year.

I was once a strawberry in a Hansel and Gretel pageant when I was in nursery school and didn't have no better sense than to dance on tiptoe with my arms in a circle over my head doing umbrella steps and being a perfect fool just so my mother and father could come dressed up and clap. You'd think they'd know better than to encourage that kind of nonsense. I am not a strawberry. I do not dance on my toes. I run. That is what I am all about. So I always come late to the May Day program, just in time to get my number pinned on and lay in the grass 'till they announce the fifty-metre dash.

I put Raymond in the little swings, which is a tight squeeze this year and will be impossible next year. Then I look around for Mr. Pearson, who pins the numbers on. I'm really looking for Gretchen if you want to know the truth, but she's not around. The park is jam-packed. Parents in hats and corsages and breast-pocket handkerchiefs peeking up. Kids in white dresses and light-blue suits. The parkees unfolding chairs and chasing the rowdy kids from Lenox as if they had no right to be there. The big guys with their caps on backwards, leaning against the fence swirling the basketballs on the tips of their fingers, waiting for all these crazy people to clear out the park so they can play. Most of the kids in my class are carrying bass drums and glockenspiels and flutes. You'd think they'd put in a few bongos or something for real like that.

Then here comes Mr. Pearson with his clipboard and his cards and pencils and whistles and safety pins and fifty million other things he's always dropping all over the place with his clumsy self. He sticks out in a crowd because he's on stilts. We used to call him Jack and the Beanstalk to get him mad. But I'm the only one that can outrun him and get away, and I'm too grown for that silliness now.

"Well, Squeaky," he says, checking my name off the list and handing me number seven and two pins. And I'm thinking he's got no right to call me Squeaky, if I can't call him Beanstalk.

"Hazel Elizabeth Deborah Parker," I correct him and tell him to write it down on his board.

"Well, Hazel Elizabeth Deborah Parker, going to give someone else a break this year?" I squint at him real hard to see if he is seriously thinking I should lose the race on purpose just to give someone else a break. "Only six girls running this time," he continues, shaking his head sadly like it's my fault all of New York didn't turn out in sneakers. "That new girl should give you a run for your money." He looks around the park for Gretchen like a periscope in a submarine movie. "Wouldn't it be a nice gesture if you were...to ahhh..."

I give him such a look he couldn't finish putting that idea into words. Grown-ups got a lot of nerve sometimes. I pin number seven to myself and stomp away. I'm so burnt. And I go straight for the track and stretch out on the grass while the band winds up with "Oh, the Monkey Wrapped His Tail Around the Flag Pole," which my teacher calls by some other name. The man on the loudspeaker is calling everyone over to the track and I'm on my back looking at the sky, trying to pretend I'm in the country, but I can't, because even grass in the city feels hard as sidewalk, and there's just no pretending you are anywhere but in a "concrete jungle" as my grandfather says.

The twenty-metre dash takes all of two minutes 'cause most of the little kids don't know no better than to run off the track or run the wrong way or run smack into the fence and fall down and cry. One little kid, though, has got the good sense to run straight for the white ribbon up ahead so he wins. Then the second-graders line up for the thirty-metre dash and I don't even bother to turn my head to watch 'cause Raphael Perez always wins. He wins before he even begins by psyching the runners, telling them they're going to trip on their shoelaces and fall on their faces or lose their shorts or something, which he doesn't really have to do since he is very fast, almost as fast as I am. After that is the forty-metre dash which I used to run when I was in first grade. Raymond is hollering from the swings 'cause he knows I'm about to do my thing 'cause the man on the loudspeaker has just announced the fifty-metre dash, although he might just as well be giving a recipe for angel food cake 'cause you can hardly make out what he's saying for the static. I get up and slip off my sweat pants and then I see Gretchen standing at the starting line, kicking her legs out like a pro. Then as I get into place I see that ole Raymond is on line on the other side of the fence, bending down with his fingers on the ground just like he knew what he was doing. I was going to yell at him but then I didn't. It burns up your energy to holler.

Every time just before I take off in a race, I always feel like I'm in a dream, the kind of dream you have when you're sick with fever and feel all hot and weightless. I dream I'm flying over a sandy beach in the early morning sun, kissing the leaves of the trees as I fly by. And there's always the smell of apples, just like in the country when I was little and used to think I was a choo-choo train, running through the fields of corn and chugging up the hill to the orchard. And all the time I'm dreaming this, I get lighter and lighter until I'm flying over the beach again, getting blown through the sky like a feather that weighs nothing at all. But once I spread my fingers in the dirt and crouch over the Get on Your Mark, the dream goes and I am solid again and am telling myself,

Squeaky you must win, you must win, you are the fastest thing in the world, you can even beat your father up Amsterdam if you really try. And then I feel my weight coming back just behind my knees then down to my feet then into the earth and the pistol shot explodes in my blood and I am off and weightless again, flying past the other runners, my arms pumping up and down and the whole world is quiet except for the crunch as I zoom over the gravel in the track. I glance to my left and there is no one. To the right, a blurred Gretchen, who's got her chin jutting out as if it would win the race all by itself. And on the other side of the fence is Raymond with his arms down to his side and the palms tucked up behind him, running in his very own style, and it's the first time I ever saw that and I almost stop to watch my brother Raymond on his first run. But the white ribbon is bouncing toward me and I tear past it, racing into the distance 'till my feet with a mind of their own start digging up footfulls of dirt and brake me short. Then all the kids standing on the side pile on me, banging me on the back and slapping my head with their May Day programs, for I have won again and everybody on 151st Street can walk tall for another year.

"In first place..." the man on the loudspeaker is clear as a bell now. But then he pauses and the loudspeaker starts to whine. Then static. And I lean down to catch my breath and here comes Gretchen walking back, for she's overshot the finish line too, huffing and puffing with her hands on her hips, taking it slow, breathing in steady time like a real pro and I sort of like her a little for the first time. "In first place..." and then three or four voices get all mixed up on the loudspeaker and I dig my sneaker into the grass and stare at Gretchen who's staring back, we both wondering just who did win. I can hear old Beanstalk arguing with the man on the loudspeaker and then a few others running their mouths about what the stopwatches say. Then I hear Raymond yanking at the fence to call me and I wave to shush him, but he keeps rattling the fence like a gorilla in a cage like in them gorilla movies, but then like a dancer or something he starts climbing up nice and easy but very fast. And it occurs to me, watching how smoothly he climbs hand over hand and remembering how he

19

looked running with his arms down to his side and with the wind pulling his mouth back and his teeth showing and all, it occurred to me that Raymond would make a very fine runner. Doesn't he always keep up with me on my trots? And he surely knows how to breathe in counts of seven 'cause he's always doing it at the dinner table, which drives my brother George up the wall. And I'm smiling to beat the band 'cause if I've lost this race, or if me and Gretchen tied, or even if I've won, I can always retire as a runner and begin a whole new career as a coach with Raymond as my champion. After all, with a little more study I can beat Cynthia and her phony self at the spelling bee. And if I bugged my mother, I could get piano lessons and become a star. And I have a big rep as the baddest thing around. And I've got a roomful of ribbons and medals and awards. But what has Raymond got to call his own?

So I stand there with my new plans, laughing out loud by this time as Raymond jumps down from the fence and runs over with his teeth showing and his arms down to the side, which no one before him has quite mastered as a running style. And by the time he comes over I'm jumping up and down so glad to see him— my brother Raymond, a great runner in the family tradition. But of course everyone thinks I'm jumping up and down because the men on the loudspeaker have finally gotten themselves together and compared notes and are announcing "In first place—Miss Hazel Elizabeth Deborah Parker." (Dig that.) "In second place— Miss Gretchen P. Lewis." And I look over at Gretchen wondering what the "P" stand for. And I smile. 'Cause she's good, no doubt about it. Maybe she'd like to help me coach Raymond; she obviously is serious about running, as any fool can see. And she nods to congratulate me and then smiles. And I smile. We stand there with this big smile of respect between us. It's about as real a smile as girls can do for each other, considering we don't practise real smiling every day, you know, 'cause maybe we are too busy being flowers or strawberries instead of something honest and worthy of respect...you know...like being people.

THE GREATEST VICTORY

F r a n k   O ' R o u r k e

I've watched a lot of them come and go these twenty years, each man possessing his own individual talent or mark of greatness: Old Diz going out that last afternoon against the Yankees with nothing on the ball but hope and heart, the Babe calling his shot in Chicago and the ball going, going into the stands while the crowd was silent and then roaring out in sincere tribute; and Gehrig moving slowly across the half-shadowed, sun-softened grass of Yankee Stadium, the tears tracking down his brown cheeks, the silent thousands watching him go, every one of them with a lump in his throat, for there was a great man who didn't know what the word "quit" meant. But there was another who walked with them through the years and will not be remembered; yet in some way he was perhaps the greatest of them all. Each time I see a skinny little guy trudge in from the bull pen, hitch up his pants and start his wind-up, I think of Lefty Smith.

Most of us didn't know his first name; and the way I found it was rooting back in the record books and running down the pages until it popped up among the so-so boys: John A. Smith. Lefty was a small man with sloping, stooped shoulders and a head such as you see on a thousand other men, squarely common and strong-jawed, with steady blue eyes and a thinning shock of black hair, rubbing bald from twenty years under a sweaty cap and too many showers in cold, stuffy locker rooms. Just a little guy with a battered black glove and a chew of tobacco in his cheek, seen mostly for scattered, brief moments in the sun, making that long walk from the bull pen to the mound, with runners squatting on first and third and the infield waiting to give him a pat and then play ball.

I thought about Lefty as we neared St. Louis last fall. The series was a natural, a streetcar series they called it, with the Red Wings and Grays set and waiting. Lefty was number eight on the Gray pitching staff that year; he went in when the regulars were frazzled or took a turn when someone turned up with a sore arm and threw their rotation out of kilter. The boys call a guy like that "insurance," a sort of slack-taker-upper. That was how Lefty rated when the series began.

Because I'm from the Middle West myself, Nebraska, I still have a small spot in my heart for any guy who comes up to the big show from that neck of the woods; and I knew Lefty came from a little town near mine and I got to thinking about him—you know, where he started and how old he was and all those things a writer worries about. I questioned the other boys about him and got the grand total I already knew—relief pitcher for the Grays and not so hot. That was all they knew, or cared to know.

I got to thinking hard about him the day before the series opened and I went down to the Sporting News and dug up the old record books; and that was when I first felt the little jerk you get around your heart when you suddenly realize you are reading the story of a fine man, a tough story and not very pretty. It went back twenty years to that Nebraska town, to a kid with bright blue eyes and a thick black thatch of hair, dreaming big hopeful dreams about the future.

I read this dope on Lefty and then, because everything that meant something was missing, I grabbed my hat and went after him. I found him at the park with the Grays, taking their final workout before the opener. He was shagging flies in centre field and I recognized him at once because he was smaller than the others and seemed to fit and blend into the background of the ball park, as though all those years had given him a sort of natural colouring. I introduced myself and explained we were from the same county back home, and when practice broke up we walked across the infield and sat in a first-base box. I offered him a cigarette and he accepted gravely and we lit up; his face above the match was a study in age and knowledge and a generous share of understanding and pain.

I asked him about his boyhood and how he got started in baseball, and he warmed up slow, but eventually got to talking, not like so many players I've interviewed who use "I" once a sentence, but soft and pleasant, rubbing his forehead and squinting a little into the slanting sunlight as he talked. I could see a farm kid of eighteen pitching a two-bit baseball against the barn door every night and working from dawn to dark in the fields. He pitched for the town team and one day that summer they played a fast semi-pro outfit at a country fair and he was right, setting them down with three hits and fanning fifteen. The manager of the North Fork State League club was in the stands, and the next week he went up for a tryout. He was scared and plenty excited, but he turned in a nice job, nothing spectacular but steady, and the manager signed him on the spot. He pitched ten games that summer, winning eight and losing two.

It was a long road for any man to travel from that day, for baseball was in his blood and even when the breaks were bad he couldn't quit. He played with a dozen clubs, maybe more: Joplin, Moline, Houston, Kansas City, Atlanta, and in his seventh year he came up to the Blue Sox for his first shot at the big time. A guy named Clary was the Blue Sox manager. He shoved Lefty into the game the next day, without rest or a decent workout, against the Yankees. He didn't have a chance, but he pitched because he had never learned any other way; and they belted him out of the park in two innings and Clary shipped him back that night and told him he was lousy. So he went back to the minors and stayed there, pitching his heart out from coast to coast, never making headlines because he had no colour, but turning in good dependable jobs.

He was just the ninth guy in the batting line-up and when he won a ball game the writers would say that Smith pitched nicely and won with excellent support, and then rave on about the hitters.

When the war came he was thirty-eight and too old to volunteer, so he quit baseball and went back to his farm to grow crops for victory. He was married, he told me, to his childhood sweetheart; and he showed me a picture of her and their two boys, ages eighteen and fifteen. She was a sweet-faced woman and the boys were stocky and had curly hair and big ears, just like his. He told me the older boy was in the Navy and the other one a senior in high school. He had this farm back in the hills, a good quarter section bought the hard way, with money saved through those long years of pitching his arm off in a bunch of whistle stops for peanut money. He didn't say that, of course, but you could tell he was proud of his family and that farm. I know—my father was a farmer and you know how a man feels about his own land. Anyway, he had been out three years when Gerrity, the Gray's new manager, made a personal trip out and asked him to sign with the Grays as relief pitcher and general adviser for the young kids on the club. Lefty wrote his older boy, the one in the Navy, and asked what he thought; and the boy wrote him to go ahead, that he'd be proud to tell all the guys on his cruiser about his father helping to keep the game they all loved going strong until they came home. So he signed with the Grays; he was forty-one years old, just my age.

I said, "How do you feel about being in a series, Lefty?"

He grinned shyly. "Kinda funny," he said quietly. "I never thought I'd make it. I wouldn't of, you understand, if it wasn't for the war."

"But you're here," I said, "and that counts. Do you think you'll get a chance on the mound?"

He shook his head slowly. "I doubt it. I'm the last man Mike would use. You understand that, don't you? I'd like nothing better, but Mike don't think I can last." He paused and then said softly, "Clary is managing the Red Wings, you know."

"Sure," I said. "Clary manages the Red Wings. What about it, Lefty?"

Then I remembered and I could feel that little quiver in his voice, that feeling of intense longing built up over the years, when he thought about taking his turn in the series and at last knowing how a man felt when he stepped on the rubber in the biggest game a man can pitch. "Yes," he said calmly, "it sure would be something for the kids to remember."

We talked a little more and he thanked me for saying hello and invited me out to the farm when I got home for a visit; and I said I'd be glad to and we shook hands and he walked across the infield to the locker room, a little guy in a big ball park. I watched him and somehow or other I felt something tugging around inside like the day I saw Gehrig take that same walk; and it came to me then that Lefty had the same love for the game in his bones that Lou had. And Lou will never be forgotten and nobody will remember this little guy. I felt bad, I don't know why, riding uptown to the hotel.

The series got under way and in the excitement and pressure of writing up games, I forgot about Lefty Smith. You remember how it went; good baseball for wartime and plenty close. They came down the line together and suddenly we were in the seventh day, all squared off at three games apiece, with the sun shining down on Memorial Park and thirty-eight thousand fans packed together like sardines, waiting for the National Anthem and that first ball. Lefty hadn't been in the first six games, but I saw him warming up in the bull pen every day, and then someone else would get the call and he would sit down and wipe the sweat from his face and wait and watch.

But today we were sitting in the pressbox and the talk was centred on just one question: who in Hades was Mike Gerrity going to pitch. He had used five of them the day before in a desperate try for No. 4, but the Red Wings blew them down and won going away; and today, with the chips down, he didn't have a man left. Clary, the Red Wing manager, was pitching Morton O'Conner for the third time. We all knew the big boy would go the route because he had strength and plenty of heart.

But the Grays? The starting pitcher hadn't been announced

and it was fifteen minutes before game time. We reviewed the list for the tenth time and made our guesses. My good friend Jim Becker, of the Express, was thinking out loud: "Galvin, no soap. Jackson, can't hold them. King, with a sore arm. Potts, too tired from yesterday. Malone, tried yesterday," and so on down the line.

"What about Lefty Smith?" I asked.

"Smith?" Jim said. "Who the devil is Smith? Oh, that old guy. He's just window dressing. Too old, too stiff, no stuff."

"Ever watch him work?" I asked.

"No," Jim said, "but the record shows, doesn't it? He's relief pitcher and he couldn't last nine. They only used him eight times this year."

"Maybe," I said, thinking about a boy throwing a two-bit baseball against a barn door. "Who, then?"

"I don't know," Jim said. "Probably he'll start Potts and hope for the best."

That was how it shaped up. Gerrity started Potts and we stood up for The Star-Spangled Banner, with the service men and women saluting our flag proudly and everyone quiet and sober-faced for in this moment we thought of the war and all those guys, our friends, listening to this game from every part of the world; and then the umps called, "Play ball!" and Morton O'Conner took the sign from his brother behind the plate, nodded, and served the first one up to Grady and we were away. It took just one inning to see how this would go.

Morton O'Conner set the Grays down in order and Potts took the mound and got ready for Littleton. The Orangetown boy singled to right, Hopper laid down a drag bunt and beat it out, and Music tripled to the right-field wall before our seats were warm. And there it was, a first-inning break and the Red Wings running wild with no one warmed up in the Gray bull pen. Gerrity called time and they gathered around Potts and I wondered who he would call in, for it was a cinch Potts was off today. Then I looked toward the right-field bull pen and saw a small figure pick up a black glove and start the long walk to the mound.

"Who the heck?" Jim asked, shading his eyes.

"Smith," I said. "Lefty Smith."

And then I thought about his wife and those two fine boys listening in and I didn't feel very good. What a break for a guy, coming in with two runs across, a man on third and nobody out, and no time for a warm-up. Twenty years to reach this moment and it might end before he had a chance really to taste its sweetness. For I knew, and Jim knew, what Gerrity was thinking. He didn't have time to warm anyone else up, so he took the long chance and called on Lefty, hoping the little guy could pitch all out for a few minutes until King or Malone got loose.

"Lord!" Jim said. "This thing is going to be terrible. The lamb to the slaughter. Look at the little guy. They'll murder him."

He did look small, coming across the infield, that big black glove hanging down and his shoulders stooped inside the loose shirt. Gerrity said something to him and they all patted him on the back, and you could see that those Grays really liked him. He took his five warm-up tosses and stepped behind the mound for the signal. He picked up the rosin bag and dried his fingers, dropped it, got the sign from Haywood, and rubbed his nose. Walker O'Conner was waiting, his big bat poised, and no one was deadlier than the Red Wing catcher with ducks on the pond. I wondered if Lefty was nervous out there, and then I knew he was the calmest man in the ball park. I held my thumbs and said a short, silent prayer for him. I was almost afraid to look. I'd never watched him pitch and I didn't know what to expect.

He stretched and glanced over toward Music and threw; it was quick and effortless and he followed through beautifully. And I knew I was seeing the result of twenty years' experience, probably the only man who appreciated the beauty of his style. The ball moved toward Walker O'Conner and dipped suddenly, taking an inside corner with the sweetest hook I'd seen in years. Walker O'Conner watched it for a called strike and rubbed dirt on his hands. He stepped in again, but this time you could tell he had more respect for the little guy on the mound. And then I had that funny feeling. I swear I looked down on Lefty Smith and felt that something great was going to happen. I remembered what he had said about wanting to win, that day before the series in the first-base box.

He struck Walker O'Conner out on four pitched balls, and Kubisky, always tough, broke his back on a slow curve and popped to Johnson at short; and then Martin, riding a terrific hitting streak, went down swinging and the crowd woke up. I looked at Jim and said, "Never heard of Smith, huh?"

"Take it easy," Jim said, but I saw the light in his eyes. "The little guy can't last. Look, Malone is warming up."

Maybe he couldn't last, but the innings began marching past and he stayed in there, trudging out to that mound, hitching up those saggy pants, and throwing with all his skill and cunning; and the Red Wings popped out and hit weak rollers and went away from the plate cussing and banging their bats on the ground. And then we were in the seventh and the score was still two to nothing, and I tried to keep my voice steady when I said, "Jim?"

Jim said, "Yeah?"

"Six complete innings," I said. "Without a hit. He can't keep it up, huh?"

"I know it," Jim said, his eyes shining. "The wonderful little guy." He pounded my arm. "Listen, he can't stand this, I tell you. You know it, I know it. He's too old. He'll ruin his arm. He ought to ease up."

The Grays were up in the first of the seventh. Mullins worked Morton O'Conner for a walk. Johnson singled to centre and Mullins pulled up at second. Liebert came up and the crowd roared. The big boy swung viciously on the first pitch and then dropped a surprise bunt. Walker O'Conner got him at first but the runners moved up. Then McKay, who was hitting hard, looked at two strikes and drove a clean hit to left centre that scored both runners and knotted it up tight. Morton O'Conner blew his nose on his sleeve and retired the side; and we faced the last of the seventh with the score tied.

Lefty was working a little harder now. I could tell that by his shoulders and his breathing. But he was still pouring them

through and the Red Wings were still breaking their bats trying for a solid blow. He got them in the seventh and in the eighth and in the ninth; and then Jim was pounding my arm and yelling. "A no-hitter for him, a no-hitter," and then I realized it was actually true. The little guy had pitched a no-hitter because he came in with no one out in the first inning, and this was the first of the tenth and the Red Wings hadn't touched him. It was wonderful and beautiful and impossible, but there it was. And then I thought about that boy of his, that sailor on his cruiser in the Pacific, and how he must be feeling and how those buddies of his would be slapping his back and cheering his old man on. I wondered if he could last, if only those Grays would get him another run. Just one run, and soon.

The tenth went by, and the eleventh, and now the crowd was standing up solidly, tier after tier, and they weren't yelling now, they couldn't and the tension was building up to fever pitch; and all over the world the wires were pounding out the story and the announcers up on the roof were hoarse and excited, maybe worse than most of us. And little Lefty was walking out there for the last of the twelfth, his back wet and dark where the sweat had soaked through, his cap pulled down over those blue eyes, walking slowly to the mound and only throwing three warm-up pitches to Haywood and then stepping back to take the sign. I guess I was staring at him, I don't know, my hands putting a piece of paper into my portable, tearing it out, crumpling it up, doing the same thing over and over again. I had a feeling that he couldn't go on much longer, and if he didn't win this game I would be sick for a month. I wanted him to win so bad I could taste it myself. But not because I was a Gray fan; it wasn't that. It had nothing to do with the Grays or the Red Wings or the money or anything like that. It was just that I wanted him to win that ball game as I wanted our boys to win this war, and that was with all my heart.

You could almost feel the pressure build up in this inning. And Hopper was up, one Nebraskan facing another. Hopper took two, fouled one off, and then caught one of those sneaking curves, stepping back and chopping with a choked bat, riding it over first base for a Texas Leaguer to right field. The first hit off Lefty in eleven innings! Hopper was on first and Music came up and he was anxious, you could see it, and long overdue. He looked at four pitches, two strikes and two balls, and I knew the Red Wings had orders to wait him out as long as they could, making him tire that arm to the very limit. Music took a third ball and a long sigh ran around the park. Music leaned back and then in, and little Lefty stretched, looked at Hopper, and threw it down the alley. Music swung and you heard the crack, and the ball was a streak over second base and Hopper was running like the wind, around second and into third standing up.

Walker O'Conner came up and I looked down at the Gray dugout. Gerrity was not coming out. Malone and King were warming up. I thought, *Leave him there, Gerrity, leave him in there. Let him play the string out, let him have it one way or the other.* And I guess Gerrity must have been thinking my way, for he didn't make a move. Lefty took the sign and stepped on the mound. He walked Walker O'Conner purposely and the bags were full. The Gray infield drew in close and you could hear their voices, husky now but strong, encouraging Lefty, helping him all they could. Kubisky was up.

Lefty struck him out. It was beautiful. On three balls. Three vicious screw balls, such as Hubbell used to throw when the chips were down, coming in and fading away like a bullet. You couldn't hear yourself talk; no one was sitting now. They were up on the seats. Martin stepped in.

Lefty struck him out. On five balls. Slower now, bent over. Three more screw balls and two blinding fast ones pulled from only God knows where. I heard a crash beside me. Jim had smashed his folding chair with his feet and didn't know it. He was holding his portable and looking down at Lefty, and he was yelling with the rest of us.

Sanderson stepped in and the Gray infield moved back and the outfield went deep and the pitchers stopped warming up in the bull pen to watch with everyone else. It was on the little man now, on him and the big boy at the plate; and I don't think that anyone in the park wished for a hit, not even the Red Wings themselves, deep down inside.

For Lefty was tired, so tired you could see it from where we stood. He was rubbing his fingers on the rosin bag and his steps were painfully slow. He took off his glove and rubbed the ball and took the sign. I knew there wasn't a thing left in his arm. There couldn't be. Not after those long innings; not after twenty years. Maybe a couple of throws, no more. I hoped he had something, just three more good ones. He didn't look at the runners; he stepped on the rubber and wound up slowly and the arm came down and the ball went in.

There was a moment then while the ball was in flight to the plate and Sanderson was crouched, the bat poised, motionless, and Haywood was waiting, his big mitt stuck up like a black box, and the crowd silent, not a cry, not a word, and the outfielders and infielders waiting, hands on knees, a moment when everything stood still or seemed to, and you could almost feel the hope in everyone as they wished that pitch past Sanderson. And then the bat swung and the sound was clear and final.

The ball went over Lefty's head and he threw up one arm in a desperate stab; his fingers touched the ball and you could hear the "flup" and then it was going into centre field and dropping, and Hopper was streaking across the plate; and I saw Lefty standing there, the glove on the ground behind him where the drive had knocked it off his hand. He was rubbing his numbed fingers and you could see the smile on his face. That was the greatness in him, the greatness that had been there all the time, all through those long years; he was smiling and the game was over and the silence still hung for a moment.

And then Sanderson was running from first base and shaking his hand and the Grays and the Red Wings were pouring out on the field around that little man and all of them were shaking his hand and trying to pat his back, and I knew that Sanderson was saying he was sorry, you could tell by his face, and the little man was smiling still and finally he came through the players, heading for the locker room; and then, all at once, you could hear the roar start and gather force, the way it did the day Babe hit that one in Chicago, and then it rolled up and out of the park and I think they heard it in Kansas City and over in Illinois; and he took off his cap, and walked into the locker room and out of sight.

There isn't much more to tell. I saw him that night at the station when he called and asked me to see him off. He had gotten away from the autograph hounds and the others; and he stood in the station, smoking a cigarette and licking his lips. He was small when I stood beside him, smaller than I had realized. He looked like a farmer or a bank clerk in a little town. He wasn't using his left arm much and I knew it was sore as a boil. We talked about this and that, and then the announcer bawled the Kansas City train and we shook hands.

"Good luck," I said. Then I grinned. "You don't need it now, Lefty. You can write your own ticket next spring."

"No, Sam," he said mildly. "I'm through. I lost the game, but it was a good one and a fine way to bow out. Maybe a lot of folks wouldn't see it that way, but I feel like I won that game, no matter what the score was." He grinned faintly. "I sort of got even with Clary, didn't I?"

I said, "More than even, Lefty. You'll read it in my column tomorrow. Clary is always bragging how he never misses real talent. I'm going to tell the world how he shipped you back to the minors without a fair chance fifteen years ago, and what you did to him today. And listen, I still think you ought to come back next year. Your arm will be all right with a winter's rest."

He grinned and shook his head. "Something snapped in my arm when I threw that last ball to Music. I didn't have a thing on it but a prayer. The arm is done for keeps, Sam."

Then I knew he was right. I said, "Lefty, don't come back."

"How about getting out for some hunting next week?" he said. "I got some nice fat pheasants on the farm."

"You got a customer," I said.

And then he shook my hand again and was gone, walking down the ramp in the crowd and moving out of sight. I bought a cigar at the newsstand and went out to catch a taxi. I don't know what made me think of it, but standing there, waiting for a taxi to pass, I thought about courage and twenty years of work to make the grade finally; and then I grinned, thinking of those two boys and his wife, and the night was very bright.

Every day you discover new information about the people and things around you. But what do you learn about yourself? The people in these stories find out that the most important insights—the ones that change your life—come from deep inside.

THE MOST IMPORTANT DAY

Helen Keller

When she was only nineteen months old, an illness left Helen Keller blind and deaf, and therefore mute. She could understand the world by touch, taste, and smell, but she had no words to describe it. This is Helen's own story of that remarkable moment of insight when one very special teacher found an answer to her silent darkness.

The most important day I remember in all my life is the one on which my teacher, Anne Mansfield Sullivan, came to me. I am filled with wonder when I consider the immeasurable contrasts between the two lives which it connects. It was the third of March, 1887, three months before I was seven years old.

On the afternoon of that eventful day I stood on the porch—dumb, expectant. I had guessed vaguely from my mother's signs and from the hurrying to and fro in the house that something unusual was about to happen, so I went to the door and waited on the steps. The afternoon sun penetrated the mass of honeysuckle that covered the porch, and fell on my upturned face. My fingers lingered almost unconsciously on the familiar leaves and blossoms which had just come forth to greet the sweet Southern spring. I did not know what the future held of marvel or surprise for me. Anger and bitterness had preyed upon me continually for weeks, and a deep languor had succeeded this passionate struggle.

I felt approaching footsteps. I stretched out my hand, as I supposed, to my mother. Someone took it, and I was caught up and held close in the arms of her who had come to reveal all things to me and, more than all things else, to love me.

The morning after my teacher came she led me into her room and gave me a doll. The little blind children at the Perkins Institution had sent it, and Laura Bridgman had dressed it, but I did not know this until afterward. When I had played with it a little while, Miss Sullivan slowly spelled into my hand the word "d-o-l-l." I was at once interested in this finger play and tried to imitate it. When I finally succeeded in making the letters correctly, I was flushed with childish pleasure and pride. Running downstairs to my mother, I held up my hand and made the letters for *doll*. I did not know that I was spelling a word or even that words existed; I was simply making my fingers go in monkey-like imitation. In the days that followed I learned to spell in this uncomprehending way a great many words, among them *pin, hat, cup* and a few verbs like *sit, stand,* and *walk*. But my teacher had been with me several weeks before I understood that everything has a name.

One day while I was playing with my new doll, Miss Sullivan put my big rag doll into my lap also, spelled "d-o-l-l," and tried to make me understand that"d-o-l-l" applied to both. Earlier in the day we had had a tussle over the words "m-u-g" and "w-a-t-e-r." Miss Sullivan had tried to impress it upon me that "m-u-g" is *mug* and that "w-a-t-e-r" is *water*, but I persisted in confounding the two. In despair, she had dropped the subject for the time, only to renew it at the first opportunity. I became impatient at her repeated attempts, and seizing the new doll, I dashed it upon the floor. I was keenly delighted when I felt the fragments of the broken doll at my feet. Neither sorrow nor regret followed my passionate outburst. I had not loved the doll. In the still, dark world in which I lived, there was no strong sentiment or tenderness. I felt my teacher sweep the fragments to one side of the hearth, and I had a sense of satisfaction that the cause of my discomfort was removed. She brought me my hat, and I knew I was going out into the warm sunshine. This thought, if a wordless sensation may be called a thought, made me hop and skip with pleasure.

We walked down the path to the well house, attracted by the fragrance of the honeysuckle with which it was covered. Someone was drawing water, and my teacher placed my hand under the spout. As the cool stream gushed over one hand, she spelled into the other the word *water*, first slowly, then rapidly. I stood still, my whole attention fixed upon the motions of her fingers. Suddenly I felt a misty consciousness as of something forgotten—a thrill of returning thought—and somehow the mystery of language was revealed to me. I knew then that "w-a-t-e-r" meant the wonderful cool something that was flowing over my hand. That living word awakened my soul, gave it light, hope, joy, set it free! There were barriers still, it is true, but barriers that could in time be swept away.

I left the well house eager to learn. Everything had a name, and each name gave birth to a new thought. As we returned to the house, every object which I touched seemed to quiver with life. That was because I saw everything with the strange, new sight that had come to me. On entering the door, I remembered the doll I had broken. I felt my way to the hearth and picked up the pieces. I tried vainly to put them together. Then my eyes filled with tears, for I realized what I had done, and for the first time I felt repentance and sorrow.

THE BREAKTHROUGH

Richard Bach

IT was morning, and the new sun sparkled gold across the ripples of a gentle sea.

A short distance from shore a fishing boat chummed the water, and the word for Breakfast Flock flashed through the air, until a crowd of a thousand seagulls came to dodge and fight for bits of food. It was another busy day beginning.

But way off alone, out by himself beyond boat and shore, Jonathan Livingston Seagull was practising. Thirty metres in the sky he lowered his webbed feet, lifted his beak, and strained to hold a painful hard twisting curve through his wings. The curve meant that he would fly slowly, and now he slowed until the wind was a whisper in his face, until the ocean stood still beneath him. He narrowed his eyes in fierce concentration, held his breath, forced one...single...more...centimetre...of...curve.... Then his feathers ruffled, he stalled and fell.

Seagulls, as you know, never falter, never stall. To stall in the air is for them disgrace and it is dishonour.

But Jonathan Livingston Seagull, unashamed, stretching his wings again in that trembling hard curve—slowing, slowing, and stalling once more—was no ordinary bird.

Most gulls don't bother to learn more than the simplest facts of flight—how to get from shore to food and back again. For most gulls, it is not flying that matters, but eating. For this gull, though, it was not eating that mattered, but flight. More than anything else, Jonathan Livingston Seagull loved to fly.

This kind of thinking, he found, is not the way to make one's self popular with other birds. Even his parents were dismayed as Jonathan spent whole days alone, making hundreds of low-level glides, experimenting.

He didn't know why, for instance, but when he flew at altitudes less than half his wingspan above the water, he could stay in the air longer, with less effort. His glides ended not with the usual feet-down splash into the sea, but with a long flat wake as he touched the surface with his feet tightly streamlined against his body. When he began sliding in to feet-up landings on the beach, then pacing the length of his slide in the sand, his parents were very much dismayed indeed.

"Why, Jon, *why?*" his mother asked. "Why is it so hard to be like the rest of the flock, Jon? Why can't you leave low flying to the pelicans, the albatross? Why don't you *eat?* Son, you're bone and feathers!"

"I don't mind being bone and feathers, mom. I just want to know what I can do in the air and what I can't, that's all. I just want to know."

"See here, Jonathan," said his father, not unkindly. "Winter isn't far away. Boats will be few, and the surface fish will be swimming deep. If you must study, then study food, and how to get it. This flying business is all very well, but you can't eat a glide, you know. Don't you forget that you fly so you can eat."

Jonathan nodded obediently. For the next few days he tried to behave like the other gulls; he really tried, screeching and fighting with the flock around the piers and fishing boats, diving on scraps of fish and bread. But he couldn't make it work.

It's all so pointless, he thought, deliberately dropping a hard-won anchovy to a hungry old gull chasing him. I could be spending all this time learning to fly. There's so much to learn!

It wasn't long before Jonathan Gull was off by himself again, far out at sea, hungry, happy, learning.

The subject was speed, and in a week's practice he learned more about speed than the fastest gull alive.

From three hundred metres, flapping his wings as hard as he could, he pushed over into a blazing steep dive toward the waves, and learned why seagulls don't make blazing steep power-dives. In just six seconds he was moving one hundred kilometres per hour, the speed at which one's wing goes unstable on the upstroke.

Time after time it happened. Careful as he was, working at the very peak of his ability, he lost control at high speed.

Climb to three hundred metres. Full power straight ahead first, then push over, flapping, to a vertical dive. Then, every time, his left wing stalled on an upstroke, he'd roll violently left, stall his right wing recovering, and flick like fire into a wild tumbling spin to the right.

He couldn't be careful enough on that upstroke. Ten times he tried, and all ten times, as he passed through one hundred kilometres per hour, he burst into a churning mass of feathers, out of control, crashing down into the water.

The key, he thought at last, dripping wet, must be to hold the wings still at high speeds—to flap up to eighty and then hold the wings still.

From six hundred metres he tried again, rolling into his dive, beak straight down, wings full out and stable from the moment he passed eighty kilometres per hour. It took tremendous strength, but it worked. In ten seconds he had blurred through one hundred forty kilometres per hour. Jonathan had set a world speed record for seagulls!

But victory was short-lived. The instant he began his pull-out, the instant he changed the angle of his wings, he snapped into that same terrible uncontrolled disaster, and at one hundred forty kilometres per hour it hit him like dynamite. Jonathan Livingston Seagull exploded in midair and smashed down into a brick-hard sea.

When he came to, it was well after dark, and he floated in moonlight on the surface of the ocean. His wings were ragged bars of lead, but the weight of failure was even heavier on his back. He wished, feebly, that the weight could be just enough to drag him gently down to the bottom, and end it all.

As he sank low in the water, a strange hollow voice sounded within him. There's no way around it. I am a seagull. I am limited by my nature. If I were meant to learn so much about flying, I'd have charts for brains. If I were meant to fly at speed, I'd have a falcon's short wings, and live on mice instead of fish. My father was right. I must forget this foolishness. I must fly home to the Flock and be content as I am, as a poor limited seagull.

The voice faded, and Jonathan agreed. The place for a seagull at night is on shore, and from this moment forth, he vowed, he would be a normal gull. It would make everyone happier.

He pushed wearily away from the dark water and flew

toward the land, grateful for what he had learned about work-saving low-altitude flying.

But no, he thought. I am done with the way I was, I am done with everything I learned. I am a seagull like every other seagull, and I will fly like one. So he climbed painfully to thirty metres and flapped his wings harder, pressing for shore.

He felt better for his decision to be just another one of the Flock. There would be no ties now to the force that had driven him to learn, there would be no more challenge and no more failure. And it was pretty, just to stop thinking, and flying through the dark, toward the lights above the beach.

Dark! The hollow voice cracked in alarm. *Seagulls never fly in the dark!*

Jonathan was not alert to listen. It's pretty, he thought. The moon and the lights twinkling on the water, throwing out little beacon-trails through the night, and all so peaceful and still....

Get down! Seagulls never fly in the dark! If you were meant to fly in the dark, you'd have the eyes of an owl! You'd have charts for brains! You'd have a falcon's short wings!

There in the night, thirty metres in the air, Jonathan Livingston Seagull—blinked. His pain, his resolutions, vanished.

Short wings. *A falcon's short wings!*

That's the answer! What a fool I've been! All I need is a tiny little wing, all I need is to fold most of my wings and fly on just the tips alone! *Short wings!*

He climbed six hundred metres above the black sea, and without a moment for thought of failure and death, he brought his forewings tightly in to his body, left only the narrow swept daggers of his wingtips extended into the wind, and fell into a vertical dive.

The wind was a monster roar at his head. One hundred kilometres per hour, a hundred and forty, a hundred and ninety and faster still. The wing-strain now at two hundred and twenty kilometres per hour wasn't nearly as hard as it had been at a hundred, and with the faintest twist of his wingtips he eased out of the dive and shot above the waves, a gray cannonball under the moon.

He closed his eyes to slits against the wind and rejoiced. Two hundred twenty kilometres per hour! And under control! If I dive from fifteen hundred metres instead of six hundred, I wonder how fast...

His vows of a moment before were forgotten, swept away in that great swift wind. Yet he felt guiltless, breaking the promises he had made himself. Such promises are only for the gulls that accept the ordinary. One who has touched excellence in his learning has no need of that kind of promise.

By sunup, Jonathan Gull was practising again. From fifteen hundred metres the fishing boats were specks in the flat blue water, Breakfast Flock was a faint cloud of dust motes, circling.

He was alive, trembling ever so slightly with delight, proud that his fear was under control. Then without ceremony he hugged in his forewings, extended his short, angled wingtips, and plunged directly toward the sea. By the time he passed twelve hundred metres he had reached terminal velocity, the wind was a solid beating wall of sound against which he could move no faster. He was flying now straight down, at three hundred forty kilometres per hour. He swallowed, knowing that if his wings unfolded at that speed he'd be blown into a million tiny shreds of seagull. But the speed was power, and the speed was joy, and the speed was pure beauty.

He began his pullout at three hundred metres, wingtips thudding and blurring in that gigantic wind, the boat and the crowd of gulls tilting and growing meteor-fast, directly in his path.

He couldn't stop; he didn't know yet even how to turn at that speed.

Collision would be instant death.

And so he shut his eyes.

It happened that morning, then, just after sunrise, that Jonathan Seagull fired directly through the centre of Breakfast Flock, ticking off three hundred forty kilometres per hour, eyes closed, in a great roaring shriek of wind and feathers. The Gull of Fortune smiled upon him this once, and no one was killed.

By the time he had pulled his beak straight up into the sky he was still scorching along at two hundred and fifty kilometres per hour. When he had slowed to thirty and stretched his wings again at last, the boat was a crumb on the sea, twelve hundred metres below.

His thought was triumph. Terminal velocity! A seagull at *three hundred forty kilometres per hour!* It was a breakthrough, the greatest single moment in the history of the Flock, and in that moment a new age opened for Jonathan Gull. Flying out to his lonely practice area, folding his wings for a dive from two thousand, four hundred metres, he set himself at once to discover how to turn.

A single wingtip feather, he found, moved a fraction of a centimetre, gives a smooth sweeping curve at tremendous speed. Before he learned this, however, he found that moving more than one feather at that speed will spin you like a rifle ball...and Jonathan had flown the first aerobatics of any seagull on earth.

He spared no time that day for talk with other gulls, but flew on past sunset. He discovered the loop, the slow roll, the point roll, the inverted spin, the gull bunt, the pinwheel.

When Jonathan Seagull joined the Flock on the beach, it was full night. He was dizzy and terribly tired. Yet in delight he flew a loop to landing, with a snap roll just before touchdown. When they hear of it, he thought, of the Breakthrough, they'll be wild with joy. How much more there is now to living! Instead of our drab slogging forth and back to the fishing boats, there's a reason to life! We can lift ourselves out of ignorance, we can find ourselves as creatures of excellence and intelligence and skill. We can be free! *We can learn to fly!*

WHY WAS ELENA CRYING?

Norma Fox Mazer

When I was in first grade, my teacher, Miss Dooty, liked me—not just as well as she liked every other kid in her class, but maybe even more. Yes, the truth was, she did like me more, she smiled at me very specially, let me put my nap blanket near her desk, and often stroked my head as I passed by her into the room in the morning.

She was tall—she seemed very tall to me—with long, long slender legs and soft yellow skin and long black eyes. She wore pale mustard-coloured suits in winter and pale, pale violet dresses that rustled in spring. To go to school in first grade was to enter a perfect world. Miss Dooty's world. Where I was liked *more.*

At home my parents liked me well enough, but they liked my sister, Elena, better.

"Why can't you be more like Elena?" my mother said once, exasperated at my tears over some trifle.

"I can't," I screamed, enraged at her stupidity, because of all the things I wanted in life, to be *more like Elena* topped the list. Oh, to have her large, moist, shining eyes instead of my little squinty green ones! Her thick dark hair instead of my frizzy head of curls! To have *her* temperament, *her* disposition, *her* cleverness, *her* ability to make people adore and love her! What was the *matter* with my mother? Didn't she know that if I could be more like Elena, I would, without question or hesitation?

Later my mother came into my room, when I was already half-asleep, and sat on my bed. "Carol..." She touched my head. "I'm sorry about what I said before. I didn't mean that, you know. You're fine the way you are. You're you, and I shouldn't have said that."

"Mmm." I bumped my head into her hip, nuzzling. I didn't blame her for what she'd said, and I didn't believe her now. It was nice of her to come and tell me I was fine, but we both knew better. I was a pain. A royal, tearful pain-in-the-neck.

No one ever said in so many words, *We like Elena better than Carol,* but there it was—something we all knew anyway. Just the way we knew that Max, our dachshund, our waddly hot dog, had a nasty habit of snooping through the garbage for the most disgusting, putrid things he could find, which he would then snap down with satisfaction.

"Ugh, Max, you old disgusting thing," someone would say, at least once a day. Just as, to me, someone would be sure to say, "Carol, are you crying *again?*"

The *faucet,* they called me. The *leaky* faucet. My mother said if someone looked at me cross-eyed, I'd cry. It was true I cried more easily than anyone I knew and on all sorts of occasions. It was a thing I hated in myself, a part of me totally out of control. The moment I got the least bit excited, or sad, or worried, the tears came. My eyes filled, my nose stuffed up, I blubbered, and the tears ran.

I never thought it was wrong that my parents liked Elena more than me. It wasn't only that she never cried. She was also older, prettier, smarter, and, without doubt, a *much* nicer person. For instance, Elena helped my mother in the house without complaining, whereas I always grouched and moaned bitterly at the least suggestion of housework. Elena was fun to be around, she had a gorgeous smile, and she was generous with her things and about other people. On mornings after she had stayed over-night with a friend, and my parents and I were forced to share the breakfast table alone, all of us sighed and glanced around morosely, missing Elena.

Yes, Max was our garbage-hound, and I was our crybaby, and Elena—oh, Elena! Elena was our princess. That was what one of my uncles called her. "Hello, Princess," he'd say, and whenever he did, I seemed to see a kind of light shining out from her head and her hands. I did love Elena's hands; they were, like all her skin, the colour of honey, and long and strong.

I don't want to give the wrong idea. Of course, Elena was normal—she also fretted over things, fought with me, and even annoyed my parents once in a while. But, for the most part, she was Elena, a shining special person.

And I was Carol, sometimes giggler, most often weeper and moaner. P.I.T.N. Pain-in-the-neck. I wondered that Miss Dooty could like me so much. She called me *gigglepot*. Her regard was a sweet, sweet mystery, and all that year I was in first grade, I hardly ever cried. Certainly not at all in school.

In second grade everything changed. My teacher, Chelia Woodenhead, did not like me *more*, or even a little bit better, than anyone else. That was all right at first, because Chelia Woodenhead seemed to be emotionless toward the whole restless lot of us. She spoke in a neutrally pitched, but firm, voice to everyone alike.

"Boy and girls, my name is Chelia Woodenhead. You will call me Miss Woodenhead. You will raise your hand when you want to speak. You will not leave your seats without permission."

Chelia Woodenhead was younger and prettier than Miss Dooty. She wore her hair down around her shoulders rather than pinned back in a knot as Miss Dooty had. She had a different pretty dress every day and even several pairs of wonderful tinted-lensed glasses, which she wore for marking our papers.

And then there was her mouth, like the rest of her—full, even lush and pretty. But when she wasn't speaking, this mouth was kept bitten together. I don't mean her lips were firmly pressed together, or that her mouth was set in a stern line. I mean her mouth was *bitten* together; there was a gathering and a puckering and a tightening and a tensing of her mouth, teeth, chin, and jaws that changed her whole face. I never knew if I was more frightened of her speaking or silent.

Well, there were her lips and the way she held them that I found terrifyingly fascinating, and there was her name, which I found deliriously funny. Woodenhead! I had only to say that name to myself, and the giggles would erupt. Woodenhead! The more I said it, the funnier it sounded. At home I said it to Elena, "Woodenhead!" and collapsed into fits of giggling. Elena joined in and both of us chanted, "Woodenhead! Woodenhead!" until Elena remembered she was four years older than I and ought to be more dignified.

All that first week in second grade, every time someone raised a hand and said, "Miss Woodenhead," I began to snort and sniffle, trying to cover my giggles.

And Miss Woodenhead began to pick me out from the other quieter, less erratic children. "Carol Wolpe, I do not think you're paying attention." "Carol, have you done your writing practice?" "Carol *Wolpe,* are you *giggling* again?"

Miss Woodenhead's voice chilled me. It was a cold north wind that might have told the experienced or the wary that a storm was coming. Still in the summer dream of Miss Dooty's affection, still being *the gigglepot,* I was unprepared.

"Miss Woodenhead," someone said. It was Friday afternoon. It was late. I was restless, dozy, dreamy, sleepy, giggly. I giggled.

"Carol Wolpe. What are you snickering about?"

"Uh, uh, uh," I said, trying not to laugh. "Uh, uh, nothing."

"Nothing, *Miss Woodenhead.*"

"Nothing, Miss Woodenhead," I parroted, choking back another volcano of giggles at the sound of her name on my lips.

"How does one laugh at nothing, Carol?"

"I don't know."

"I don't know, Miss *Woodenhead.*"

"I don't know, *Miss Woodenhead,*" I repeated, the dangerous giggles still foaming at the corners of my mouth. Oh, silly Carol, swallow them back! Press your lips together! Make a mouth like Chelia Woodenhead's!

"Don't be smart with me!"

"Smart?" I repeated.

"I do not like children who mock me."

"Mock you?"

"Like *that*!"

"Like what?" I said. No longer giggling.

"Carol Wolpe. Come here."

I rose from my seat. I walked to the front of the room and stood in front of Miss Woodenhead.

"I will tell you again. I do not like children who mock me."

My head swung back and forth. "I'm not mocking you." My heart, like my head, seemed to swing loosely, back and forth inside my chest. "I'm not mocking you," I bleated.

"Use my name."

"Miss Woodenhead."

"Stand up straight! Now tell me—*what were you laughing about?*"

I no longer knew. Had I been laughing? Nothing seemed at all funny now.

"Speak up," she ordered.

I stared at her numbly. Speak up about *what?* I had lost the drift of this dialogue, had forgotten where, or why, it had begun. I was only, finally, aware that I was in dirty, dangerous waters. The rest of the class knew it, too. There was that kind of waiting stillness that comes over kids when one of them is in danger from a teacher. It's a stillness made up of relief that someone else is the target, uneasiness that at any moment the teacher might shift gears and attack *you*, and pleasure in watching another lamb being devoured.

Yes, that was exactly the way I felt by then, as if I were being devoured by the luscious lips of Chelia Woodenhead. I couldn't drag my gaze away from those lips.

"Look at me," she said. "Look me in the eyes!"

I did, but only for a moment, then *my* eyes dropped like a plummet to her lips, those lips. I felt compelled to watch them, as you might watch a pair of lunatic dogs, chained, but straining to reach you.

"You are a sneaky, shifty child, Carol Wolpe." This pronouncement was delivered in the same neutral tone of authority in which she informed us that two times two was four. A fact. A given. A piece of information without which we could not pass through second grade.

"Well?" Miss Woodenhead demanded.

What did she want now? What was I supposed to say? How act? "Yes," I said, thinking that might be safe.

"Yes, what?"

"Yes, Miss Woodenhead," I quivered

"Yes, Miss Woodenhead," she repeated. "What does *that* mean?"

"I don't know," I said. "I don't *know*!" And I began to cry. I cried bitterly, without reservation, howls and wails of terror and outrage. There—at that moment—was where my crying career began again. After that, for years, so far as I can remember, I cried at every turn.

Of course, I was doomed in second grade. It was misery. So much misery that, as often as possible, I had a sore throat, a stomachache, a headache, or anything else that, by the grace of God, could make me an invalid for a day or two. And if I was very lucky and had been good (meaning no tears or storms for at least a day), my mother often let me spend those blessed, Woodenhead-less days in Elena's room.

My room was bigger than hers, but hers was special. Tucked under the staircase to the attic, it had a sloping wall covered with faded wallpaper showing tiny ladies in blue ballgowns and tiny gentlemen in little white wigs and black ties dancing about with their hands daintily held in the air. I thought it was the most wonderful wall in the world, and if I stared hard enough at the tiny ladies and the tiny gentlemen, I would hear music and see them dance.

They took only the teeniest, tiniest steps, but they were all smiling and happy, and they said things to each other like, "Isn't it a dee-*light*ful day, Mr. Gorham-Atekins?" And "I do believe you are charming my heart, Miss Maxwell-Vandersniff."

Not only did Elena have Mr. Gorham-Atekins and Miss Maxwell-Vandersniff dancing perpetually on the wonderful sloping wall, but she also had a special window. Like all the other windows in the house, *my* windows were square, they had two panes of glass, they went up and down and sometimes they broke or cracked. Elena's window did all those things, too, but besides that it was set *into* the wall so that, instead of a window *sill*, she had a window *seat*. There was a cushion on the window seat, and to be allowed to sit there, reading, and eating a chocolate bar, on a rainy day was a privilege I rated only slightly below being asked to come into bed with Elena and tell her stories.

I had two basic kinds of stories in my repertoire—ghost stories and love stories. Now this was interesting. *I* never cried when I told my stories, but Elena nearly always did, usually at the point where I either killed off my character (ghost story), or condemned her to forever roam the world (love story), always just missing her beloved. "Oh, how *sad*," Elena would sniffle. But things like that never drew a tear from me.

One year, in fifth grade, we were asked to write a composition on "The Most Wonderful Person I Know." I sat for five stricken minutes while, all around me, people bent to their papers. Then my hand went up. "Yes, Carol?" "Miss Clements—" My voice quivered, my eyes were wet. "I don't know who to write about." "Of course you do," she said briskly. *No, I didn't.*

While I could make up stories easily for Elena, inventing fabulous happenings, school was different. School was *marks*. It meant being judged. It meant that cold snake in the centre of my belly that had taken up residence in second grade and never left me. In school I didn't believe in myself, in what I could do, or that I could do *anything* praiseworthy. So, usually, I didn't do much.

My eyes swam. My nose twitched like a rabbit's. Then my friend, Bernie, poked me. "Write about your sister," she hissed. What relief. Of course! Elena *was* "The Most Wonderful Person I Know." I began, "My sister—" Simply writing those two words made my heart fill like a sponge absorbing water.

"Good for you!" Miss Clements wrote on my paper. "Why can't you always do work like this? Reminds me of your sister." All through grade school, junior high, and into high school, every teacher *I* had , had been *Elena's* teacher four years previously. And had not forgotten her.

"Wolpe?" the teacher would say on the first day. "Related to Elena Wolpe?"

"Elena's my *sister.*"

A nod, a smile, sometimes a congratulatory "Oh, very good, very good." After a while, I realized the teachers were congratulating themselves: they thought they were going to be lucky enough to have another Elena Wolpe in their classrooms. Instead, they got me.

I always started out the school year meaning to be like Elena, tearless, cooperative, smart, willing, and pleasant, but, somehow, before long, things became hopelessly fouled up. My teachers shook their heads. No Elena Wolpe, just another problem student.

"If only you'd try harder," Mr. Rideau, my eighth-grade history teacher, said to me once when I handed in a paper two weeks late.

"Yes," I said, my eyes filling, *"I will."*

"You told me the same thing weeks ago," he pointed out.

"I'll try," I said, blinking hard. Oh, please don't let me cry, I prayed. *Please.* "I'm sure I'll do better, Mr. Rideau." I fled before my traitorous tear ducts betrayed me again.

All my promises were given in utter sincerity. It was just that things happened. They happened *to* me, I felt, just as *tears* happened to me. I *meant* to do my work on time. I *always* meant to. I wrote down all the assignments and took the books home, but then, somehow, it was so *hard* to just sit down and do the work. Instead I'd roam around the house, playing with poor old Max (who was now half-blind), or I'd read for a while (always promising myself that at the end of *this* chapter I'd do my homework), or go into Elena's room for a chat with Mr. Goreham-Atekins and Miss Maxwell-Vandersniff.

That year—I was fourteen—Elena's life changed. She fell in love with Mark Feingold. Mark was in college on a basketball scholarship, he was an A student, he was tall and adorable with dark hair and a sweet, shy smile. He was, if anything, a male Elena. I immediately fell passionately in love with him.

Hopeless, of course. He brought me a gift. Crayons. *Crayons* for a fourteen-year-old! I was hot with despair. Those crayons—I couldn't bring myself to throw them away—but I seemed to read my future in them. I'd *never* find someone like Mark. Who would ever take me seriously? Who would ever want *me*, an endlessly leaking faucet?

Walking home one day, I heard, ahead of me, two girls discussing a third girl. They agreed that everyone liked this other girl. They did, too, but *why*? What was her magic? How did she attract and keep so many friends?

"She's so pretty," said one.

"Yes, but it's not that. Kathi is prettier. No, it's because she's nice to everyone."

"And not in a phony way."

"She always acts glad to see you."

"Yes, and not stuck up about how pretty she is and how much everyone likes her."

I *knew* it was Elena they were talking about. I rushed up. "Are you talking about Elena Wolpe?" They looked at me coolly. Who was this grungy little eavesdropper?" "That's my sister." Now they looked at me again, differently. *This* is Elena Wolpe's sister? Elena, the beautiful and fair and good? They smiled cynically.

"She is too my sister," I shouted, and to my horror—but not surprise—my throat swelled, my eyes overflowed, and then I was *crying in public.* How I hated my tears! Despised them! Prayed to God night after night to make me a miracle, dry up my tears, turn me into a calm, tearless, radiant person like Elena.

I began to keep a calendar. For every day that passed tearless I crayoned in a large gold star. For every other day, an even larger, midnight blue, upside-down *T.* But it was my worst time of all. Worse, even, than second grade and Chelia Woodenhead. I could not get out of my head how *perfect* Elena was and how unperfect, flawed, and *hopeless* I was. I was miserable and so I cried. I cried rivers, lakes, oceans. If I woke up in the middle of the night, I'd think of Elena and Mark and cry. And in the morning, looking at my swollen eyes, it was all I could do not to cry again.

I *wanted* to stop crying. I not only hated my tears, I even hated anyone else's tears. In the movies if I saw a character crying on screen, while others around me sniffled sympathetically, I was overcome with disgust. I couldn't bear to read a crying scene in a book. I'd throw it across the room and refuse to read another page. But after only two months I tore up the calendar, sick of crayoning in only upside-down *T*s.

I tore each page of my calendar in half and then in half again, and then into confetti and threw it all over the floor. My mother passed my room. "What in the world—?"

"Never mind! Leave me alone!" My mother sighed and withdrew.

Then Elena came, carrying Max. "Carol, couldn't you be nicer to Mom?"

I tore up June. Bits of paper floated everywhere, settling on my bed, drifting into sneakers, mingling with the dust on shelves.

"What are you tearing up?" Elena said.

"You," I said, laughing maniacally so I wouldn't cry. "I'm tearing you up, Elena! And I ripped July crosswise and then in half again and once more, and began on August. When I was done destroying the calendar, I broke every crayon into bits, and then threw myself across the confetti-covered bed and cried. I cried because I'd torn up my calendar, which I had really liked, cried because I had demolished Mark's gift, and cried because no one understood me. (Topping the list of people who didn't understand me was *me*). And finally, of course, I cried because I was crying.

And I was so *tired* of crying. So *bored* with my crying. Why couldn't I stop? I began howling like a dog.

"What's the *matter*?" Elena said, looking in again.

"Nothing," I howled. "Shut your face!"

She sat on the bed next to me. "Are you in pain? Are you sick?"

"Nooooo!"

"Carol, Carol..."

"I want to stop *crying*," I bawled miserably.

"Well, then," Elena said in my ear, "stop."

The logic of it! I sat up as if someone had whispered the secret of the universe. I shook my head like a dog, like Max when flies bothered him. *If you don't want to cry, don't cry. Stop.* It was such a revelation. It was as if, up until that instant, I had been living in a world where such thoughts were as unreal, as powerless, as Miss Maxwell-Vandersniff and Mr. Goreham-Atekins. *They* had to go on dancing eternally. And *I* had to go on crying.

I got up, looked in the mirror at my swollen eyes and dripping nose, and thought, What if I never cried again? It scared me. What would I do instead? Pick my nose? Bang my head against the wall? *Anything*, I thought, *just stop crying*. And I remembered the eight-kilometre cross-country run for the Children's Fund last year. The final kilometre had been torture. I had cried the whole way, gasping for air, pushing one leaden leg before the other, but full of a stiff, sickening pride. I would *not* give up. I would *not* stop. I would go over the finish line, *running*. And I had. Now I felt the same sickening pride entering me. *I'll never cry again. I will not. I have stopped crying.*

A few weeks later at dinner, my father said, "I think the

faucet has stopped dripping." I went on eating. Better not to talk about my tears or lack of tears. Better to just keep running that race. I did not cry for days, for weeks, for a whole month. Stars, stars, stars.

Then came the day when Elena and Mark told us they were going to get married. Everyone was hugging everyone else. Everyone was laughing and beaming and smiling. I, too, but it was my wide-eyed, wild-eyed grin against tears. *I wanted to cry!* Oh, for a good, long, satisfying sob. Oh, to throw myself across my bed and howl. Howl for the sheer luxury of it. Could one little crying session hurt that much?

I ran to my room. I threw myself across the bed. I pounded my fists into the mattress. I sniffled and choked. I was on the verge of tears, the way someone desperate might be on the edge of a cliff, ready to throw herself over. Why not crash? Did it matter? Who would care?

I would. I sat up, grinding fists into my eyes. *Oh, no, you don't. No-you-don't-Carol-Wolpe-Ex-Crier-Champion-of-the-World.* And I didn't.

The wedding was set for June, after Elena graduated. No big affair, just the family on both sides and some friends. Mark and Elena were writing their own vows and the ceremony would be held in our backyard. For weeks, nothing but the wedding was talked about in our house. "She is glowing," my mother said to a friend. "She is absolutely glowing."

But the night before the ceremony, I heard Elena crying in her room. Elena crying? Was it some weird trick of my mind? Now that *I* wasn't crying, *Elena* was? I knocked on her door. "Elena? It's me. Can I come in?"

"Yes." Muffled.

She was sitting up straight in her maple rocker, rocking and weeping. Sympathetic prickles began in my eyes.

"Elena?" I said. "Elena, what's the *matter?*"

"Oh, Carol!" She held out her arms and I fell down on my knees and hugged her. We stayed like that for a while, hugging and rocking, Elena weeping, crying as I had never heard her

crying, and me trying like the devil to stay on the tearless wagon.

How scary it was to see Elena cry. I knew it had to be for some awful, secret, shocking reason. Was she dying of leukemia? I looked at her golden face, beautiful even covered with tears. No, she was healthier than all of us. Then had she discovered she didn't, after all, love Mark? For one instant I prepared to step into the breach. (Mark, will you marry me?) But then I thought of something even worse and nearly impossible to believe: *Mark* had changed his mind about marrying Elena. What else could possibly have brought on such torrents of tears?

"Oh, Elena," I moaned, hugging her tighter.

"Carol, Carol—I'm—so—*scared,*" she said.

"You'll find someone else," I said.

She stared at me and wiped her nose on a corner of her shirt. Elena, wiping her nose on her shirt? That was the sort of thing *Carol* did.

"You just wiped your nose on your shirt," I said.

"Why shouldn't I?" she said weepily. "You wipe your nose on *napkins,* for God's sake."

"I haven't done that for quite a while—"

"You scream and kick and rant and rave," she went on. "You think somebody's a fool, you *say* they're a fool."

"Not to their face," I said, ashamed.

"So *what*? You say it. Carol, do you realize I never say *anything* bad about *anyone*?"

"Of course you don't," I said. "That's why—"

"They all think I'm so *good,*" she said.

"You *are.*"

"Listen to me," she said. "*Listen* to me." She grabbed my arms. "I tell you I'm *scared.* Mark thinks I'm—wonderful." Her voice shook. "I love him so much, Carol. What happens when he finds out?"

"Finds out what?" I said in bewilderment.

"That I'm not *wonderful.*"

"But you are," I said again.

"Shut up!" She sat up straighter. I shut up, never having

been told to *shut up* by Elena. It just wasn't her style. "I always thought when I got older it would be different. I could just *relax*—be more like you—" My mouth fell open. Nothing came out. "—say the things I'm really thinking, not be so *nice* all the time. Nice, nice, they're always telling me how *nice* I am. I'm *not* that nice! No one is!"

I was stunned by the thought that Elena's perfection had been as much a burden to her as my crying had been to me. I wanted badly to help her, as she had helped me once. She had had the simple right words for me, but I couldn't think of a thing to say. So I just hugged her a lot more, until she said, "I'll be all right now, Carol. Thanks." I went back to my room. I wanted very much to cry, and I didn't.

The next day the weather was perfect. "Nervous?" my mother asked Elena at breakfast. She shook her head. She looked like herself again, at least the self I recognized.

So then, the wedding in our backyard. One of Mark's friends sang. My parents stood on one side of Elena and Mark, and his parents and his grandmother stood on the other side. I didn't hear too much of the ceremony. I was thinking about Elena, and I was thinking about me. About all the years behind me, and all the years ahead. About last night, and about tears and fears and other foul things.

When I looked up, Mark and Elena were kissing. They were married. My sister was a married woman. Elena, I thought, *Elena*, everything is changing.

A woman sitting next to me touched my arm. "Are you crying, dear? You're the sister of the bride, aren't you?"

"Yes," I said. "Yes, I am. *But I'm not crying.*" And indeed I wasn't.

The turn of a key. The rev of an engine, the squeal of tires.
The whistle of wind in your hair. Wheels can take us on
wonderful, even fantastic journeys—but there is always
an element of danger.

YOUNG AND IN LOVE WITH THEIR WHEELS

June Callwood

IN a few weeks the young men will be storing their motorcycles for the winter. It has been a long lovely summer, riding free on the highways in the open air, unencumbered by the confinement of an automobile, alone under sky, masters of their fate.

The young men are full of nostalgic regret as they wax the machines one last time. The men are filthy, their hands black with oil, but the motorcycles are spotless.

The young men have always loved wheels. Their first toys were cars and trucks. When they could walk, they pulled a wagon. After that came a tricycle, wooden blocks on the pedals so their little legs would reach, grumpy because they weren't allowed to cross the street.

After that the first two-wheeler and that crazy day when they learned to balance, a parent puffing alongside holding boy and bike upright while the child tipped and veered, his face a mask of fright, determination and joy.

At puberty the young men had ten-speed bicycles, a rite of passage. They could go anywhere. On Saturdays they floated to the plazas to buy an album, home with it in the back-pack, clicking softly through the gears, wind on the face.

Meanwhile money was being saved from the summer jobs cutting lawns, from the after school jobs in fast-food chains and supermarkets. The young men want motorcycles. A motorcycle has everything young men crave in order to assure themselves they are no longer boys: independence, power, mobility, sexiness, importance.

The motorcycle horrifies parents, who can't understand it and won't ride it. Another plus.

The young men are indignant at the high cost of motorcycle insurance. They invest in gadgets. They take a safety course and learn about shoulder checks. They buy leather because if somethings goes wrong and they hit the pavement, they don't want to be flayed.

The truth is that if something goes wrong and they hit the pavement, leather can be irrelevant. On impact, if the motorcyclist leaves his machine, he slams down with a force approximately that of being dropped from a building. The motorcyclist knows this will not happen to him. About 500 000 Canadians had motorcycle licences in 1982 and more than 400 died. Dying is what happens to someone else. Young men have believed that since human history began.

Sunnybrook Medical Centre in Toronto is the regional trauma unit for southern and central Ontario so it is where motorcyclists are taken if they are still breathing after the accident. Usually there is a severe head injury; helmets are not designed for high-speed collisions. Often there will be an amputation, maybe two; motorcycle accidents are the leading cause of amputations in North America.

Not infrequently, there is paralysis.

The motorcyclists weep at night in the privacy and loneliness of darkness. Their parents come to visit, grateful for such mercies as saving the other leg, one hand that still has feeling. The person in the next bed is still in a coma.

Dr. Peter Lane sorts out the injuries. He is head emergency

physician and chief trauma team leader. He admits he feels frustration, even anger, at the parents and motorcyclists who stupidly put fine young lives in deliberate jeopardy. He tries to hide his exasperation when he tells parents what the accident has done to twenty years of nurturing, of regular dental checkups, of tension over examinations, of self-doubt, of growth and howling good times.

The parents are too numb to explain. Anyway, they can't. All parents hate the motorcycles but they love the young men, and the young men love the motorcycles.

The young men who survived this summer are putting away their beloved machines. There is a ritual to be observed immaculately. The crank case must be drained and everything washed thoroughly. Little boys from the neighbourhood watch transfixed. The young man has been a god all this summer, his comings and goings full of splendid racket.

When everything has been done to an exacting standard, the young man is ready to push the heavy machine into a storage place where it will be warm all winter. He covers his motorcycle with care. It would be unbearable if next April, when the streets at last are clear of snow, the motorcycle did not start, first try.

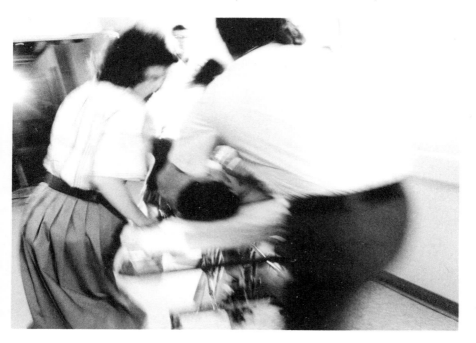

A GOOD TIME TONIGHT

Gary and Louise Hodge

The sea was glassy and the waves crashing into the Australian coast were perfect. The recent storms had built up the swell as Simon caught his last wave for the day. Riding the board was one place where he felt in total harmony with the sea. He had seen his father returning from his jog along the beach and decided to go in to meet him. His father bent over to catch his breath and rested his hands on his knees.

"Whew! I'm getting old. I used to be able to do twice that distance."

"It's your first run for some time dad. You'll get better and I reckon you'll find it easier when you get rid of that pot belly."

Simon knew that this would get a response.

"You devil. I'll give you pot belly."

His father chased him up to the parking lot, Simon struggling to keep ahead with his surfboard. As he strapped the board to the roof rack his father threw him the keys.

"You can drive back home Simon. Leave the 'learner' sign on the roof."

Simon peeled off his wet suit and quickly stepped into his jeans and pulled on a bulky sweatshirt. He had been learning to drive for over a month now with his father.

"Thanks Dad! I was hoping you'd offer." It was 7:15 a.m. The return home from the early morning jog and surf was a great way for him to get experience on the roads before the traffic built up. Living four kilometres from the beach meant driving on a highway with traffic lights and then cutting through a back street—all good practice.

As Simon let the clutch out, he experienced the thrill of being in control of a car. The powerful eight-cylinder motor moved effortlessly through the gears and he soon reached the speed limit.

"Well done mate. You're coming along nicely. But you did forget to adjust the mirror and seat."

"But I had already done that!"

"It doesn't matter—you get into the habit so that you don't forget on the day you go for your licence."

As the car drew into the driveway, Simon gave it one last rev and switched off the motor.

"Good steady driving Son, but you must learn to drive defensively. Just because the light is green your way doesn't mean some idiot isn't going to go through a red light. Keep your eyes open and don't go sailing through intersections at full speed. Slow down a touch."

It was the last day of term and life seemed pretty good. Simon sat in the car for a while and contemplated his day. First to school for tutorial then into town to buy a leather jacket for Nikki's party that night.

Mandy, his new girlfriend, was allowed to go with him even though she had been grounded by her mom for the previous two weeks. She had been caught in a nightclub by liquor detectives and had received a warning, even though she hadn't touched a drop. Mandy's great, he thought, popular, lots of personality and caring about others and what happened in the world. His parents and little sister were all going down to the beach house at Madora Bay for the weekend and he was allowed to stay on his own in the house. "Gr...Great!," he said out loud, mimicking the sound of a car rev for his own amusement.

Nikki's house was only a short distance from Mandy's. I'll really surprise her when I pick her up in Mom's car, he thought, smiling as he imagined Mandy's face. His mother always left the spare keys on a hook in the kitchen and she would never know he had taken them.

He planned to go into town during his spare and be back in time to collect his report. The first period passed more quickly than he had thought it would. On the bus into town he thought about his encounter with Mario Lavorgna. He had grabbed the ridiculous looking beanie from Mario's head as he was talking to his best mate Danny by the lockers. Mario's hair had been cut badly and there were bruises on his face. Poor guy, he thought, guessing that Mario's father was responsible. Simon found it hard to comprehend because in his own father's eyes he could do no wrong.

He walked the few blocks to the clothes store. The music blared as Simon went through the racks. The salesman, all decked out in outrageous gear, sidled up to him suspiciously, eyeing his school uniform.

"Did you want some help mate? Just take care not to mess up the display." Simon felt a rush of annoyance. He had four hundred and fifty dollars in cash in his pocket. All hard earned from pushing trolleys and restocking shelves at the supermarket on Saturday mornings all year.

"I want to buy. You got anything more interesting here than this lot?"

The salesman indicated a rack of the new season's leather gear and moved off rather obviously.

Simon found what he wanted right away. A jacket in soft black kid, which zipped up diagonally across the front. He hooked it down and tried it on in front of a mirror. Then he saw that it was designed with the zip edges continuing along the sides of the collar, so that by pulling up the zip completely the collar turned back into an interesting peaked shape high on the neck. It cost four hundred and twenty dollars. Simon knew it would look great with his black pants and grey shirt. He took it over to the salesman and put it down on the counter without a word. The man placed the jacket in a grey carrying bag, looking vexed. Simon put down the money slowly and exactly, one fifty-dollar bill at a time, relishing every moment. The whole transaction took place in silence.

As he left the shop, the salesman called out sarcastically, "Come again!"

Simon paused and looked around.

"Not if you're here mate."

With thirty bucks in his pocket, Simon decided he could do a bit of damage in town before going back to school. He'd have a snack and take in a movie. As he waited for his burger and Coke at the fast-food store he would have liked someone to talk to. He had wanted Danny to come into town with him. Danny's such a dag, but a good mate, he said to himself. I'll really impress him tonight with my driving.

Simon sank back into the comfortable seat in the cinema. The short was a boring documentary on irrigation schemes in the Punjab River in India, which drove him out into the foyer for a video game. He then went back to the movies when the main feature started. One hundred and twenty-four minutes of action and escapism. Life *was* pretty good.

He knew he had done well in his report. No sweat, he assured himself. His parents were delighted when he showed the report to them. They left around five o'clock with his little sister Kathy.

"Bye Simon!" The family waved as the car drove off down the road towards the highway.

Alone at last. Simon went into the kitchen to make sure his mother had left the car keys in the usual place. They dangled there off the cup hook, promising a good time.

He took extra care getting ready. A long shower, shampoo and conditioner, deodorant and even a bit of his father's after-shave. He approved of the image before him in the mirror. The leather jacket looked great with his black pants, as he had imagined it would.

In the car on the way to Mandy's, Simon took great care with his driving. Even when a police car pulled up alongside of him he didn't flinch. He had to suppress a desire to wave and smile at the sullen police officer sitting in the passenger seat, but realized that this could lead to suspicion. So he leaned forward and turned up the radio instead.

As he pulled in around the corner from Mandy's house, Simon felt on top of the world. His parents had given him a fifty dollar bonus for his report and here he was with the best-looking girl in the school going to Nikki's party. His parking between two stationary cars was a model of perfection. If only Dad could see me now! he boasted to himself.

Simon rang the doorbell. It was opened immediately by Mandy's little brother, Ben. Ben raced down the passage yelling, "Mandy—your boyfriend's here!" Simon was left high and dry and feeling a bit foolish. Mrs. Sokolich came to the door and apologized for Ben's behaviour.

"Sorry Simon, but he's been waiting for you to arrive. Come on in."

Mrs. Sokolich looked a bit down as she showed Simon into the lounge room. Ben's toys were all over the place and the room was in a mess.

"Would you like a juice or something?"

"No thanks Mrs. Sokolich. We'd better be going. The bus will be here soon."

Ben came charging into the room followed by Mandy. He leapt onto the sofa and pulled a pocket knife out of his belt.

"Do you want to borrow my knife? There might be some bullies at the party."

Mandy looked embarrassed by her brother's behaviour.

"Grow up Ben. You're a real pain."

Ben pulled a face and mimicked her.

"Grow up Ben. You're a real pain."

They all chose to ignore him. It was easier.

Mrs. Sokolich walked to the door with Simon and Mandy.

"Have a good time and be careful."

Mandy kissed her mother on the cheek and the front door closed behind them. As they walked to the front gate, Ben's wolf whistle followed them.

"Sometimes he's a real dag. I think he's getting out of hand. I wish Dad was still around to help a bit. You know Mom's been looking for work. I don't know what'll happen when he comes home from school and Mom's not there."

Simon glanced sideways at her. She looked great in a studded top he hadn't seen before.

"Hey—I've got a surprise for you." He steered her over in the direction of his mother's car. "It's Mom's."

"Simon, you only have a learner's permit. How come your mother let you have the car?"

"She doesn't know. She's down at the beach house all weekend."

"I don't know Simon. What if you're caught?"

"No chance. I'll drive really carefully. Listen—I drive to the beach every day. I'm ready."

Mandy looked troubled. She glanced back towards the house.

"Okay, but you're not drinking at the party."

"No way!"

Simon unlocked the passenger's door and bounced around to the driver's door. "I can't wait until I have my own car."

He took time in carefully adjusting the rearview mirror, his seat and seat belt.

"Let's go! I have to pick up Danny on the way."

"But that takes us in the opposite direction to Nikki's!"

"I promised Danny I'd pick him up. And he hasn't seen me drive yet."

Simon inserted a tape into the car's stereo system and turned up the volume.

Danny walked to the bus stop on Lissadell Street to be picked up by Simon. He could have telephoned and had Simon come straight to the house, but he liked the quiet of having the place all to himself. He wondered what it would be like without his mother and father around permanently. He tried to imagine it but couldn't.

Simon drove sedately around the corner in his mom's red Holden Astra and pulled up alongside Danny. Mandy was already in the car and was looking much older and more sophisticated than at school.

"Hi Danny," Mandy said warmly and turned around.

"Hello mate," Simon seconded.

"Hi. Let's go."

Simon was wearing his new jacket. It gave off a fresh leather smell that was somehow comforting. Danny felt at ease in the car as Simon drove carefully along. It was like a cocoon—he wished that he could be driven forever like this. The sound system in the car sounded crisp and deep as it played Simon's tape. For the first time all day everything was well in Danny's world.

Simon glanced at Danny in the rearview mirror.

"Do you want some booze? I can pull up at the liquor store if you like."

"What are you drinking?"

"Nothing. I've got some Coke and chips to take. I'm not taking any risks."

"I don't want anything to drink. My old man will be waiting for me when I get home to talk about my bad report card, so I want to be able to think straight."

The party was in full swing by the time they arrived at Nikki's house. Cars were pulling up at all angles and people were coming and going. There were lots of faces that Danny didn't recognize. He left Simon and Mandy to themselves and went looking for a glass. When he passed by Helga she called out hello and moved towards him. She seemed to be moving and talking in slow motion and Danny couldn't help but laugh.

"I'm not drunk," she tried to say, sounding upset.

Yes you are, he said mentally, and took the glass gently out of her hand. He told her that she had had enough to drink. Suddenly, Helga stumbled and fell onto the grass. A few people laughed. She was crying as he helped her to her feet and directed her back to a seat. He saw Nikki coming over to check that she was all right. Helga let out a groan and doubled over, vomiting.

Danny backed off. He felt his own stomach become uneasy. Mandy had hurried over to help Helga. Thank God, he thought.

He found a glass and took some of Simon's Coke. The party was disappointing. He just wasn't in the party mood—the thought of his father waiting for him put him off and he felt distanced from everyone. After half an hour he decided to leave quietly without saying anything. Nikki saw him going and went up to him.

"Where are you going Danny? You're not leaving already?"

"I'm going down to the Seven-Eleven to get some more Coke."

"Don't worry—there's heaps here."

"How's Helga?"

"OK now. Mandy's with her."

Danny nodded and made a move to go. Nikki tried to detain him by asking. "Hey, have you met Angie Dunne? She goes to Williamstown High and I think you'd like her."

"I'll catch you later Nikki. Thanks for everything."

Danny escaped into the cool air. As the sounds of the party receded, he welcomed the darkness of the night. The slight breeze moved the tops of the trees and cleared the smoke from his hair and clothes.

By the time he got home, the house lights were on. Danny let himself in and called out.

"Mom. Dad. I'm home."

His mother appeared in her dressing gown, her hair down and face cleaned of all her make-up. Her eyes without liner and mascara appeared small and almost colourless.

"Danny! You're home early." She looked uncomfortable and quickly looked over her shoulder to her bedroom door. "Your father has had to go to Sydney on business unexpectedly. He'll be back next Wednesday. I'm off to bed—I'm exhausted."

Danny went to his room. The house felt strange. Somehow violated. He went straight to bed and for hours listened to the rain before dropping off into a disturbed sleep.

Simon noted that the party was like any other—familiar faces and conversations. Except this time he had Mandy all night to himself. Mandy's friend Helga passed out on rum and Coke and was sick everywhere, but Mandy took time to look after her and put her to bed. Helga was a bit pathetic, Simon thought, but it showed him another side of Mandy that he liked. All his mates kept urging him to have some alcohol, green ginger wine, rum, coolers, but he refused, even though they gave him a hard time.

"No thanks. I'm not drinking tonight."

After dancing for hours, Simon looked at his watch. He felt like having some time alone with Mandy. Rain had driven them inside. Simon decided it was time to make a move.

"Let's go for a little spin before I take you home."

"What about Danny?"

"He's taken off somewhere. Been in a really strange mood. I'll catch him tomorrow. Let's go to the park, we can talk there."

Simon pulled in as far away from the other line of cars that had parked overlooking the city as he could. He turned off the motor and the headlights and they sat for a moment in silence, the city lights twinkling against the sky, causing a glow which lit up the murky grey of the clouds. Simon leant across and kissed Mandy gently. She responded and placed her arms around his shoulders. Suddenly their teeth clashed and they both laughed, rather embarrassedly.

"I'm not very experienced at this," said Mandy.

"It doesn't take long to learn," replied Simon, attempting to present himself as a person of more experience than he actually was. They kissed again and relaxed and enjoyed their first attempts at intimacy.

"You know, I've been really crazy about you for ages. How about going out steady with me?"

Mandy went silent for a short while.

"I'm sorry Simon...I really like you too, but I'm not ready just yet. Let's take it as it comes."

"Oh, come on."

"No Simon. Please don't pressure me."

Mandy wondered whether she had done the right thing and if Simon would still want to see her.

"If I don't, do you still want to see me?" she asked tentatively.

"Of course I want to. I think you're great! Hey, how about a movie tomorrow?"

"I have to help my mom around the house on Saturdays, but the five o'clock show would be O.K."

Mandy looked at the illuminated light on the car's dashboard. 1:55 a.m. "I think I'd better be getting home Simon."

They kissed again, and Simon felt on top of the world. It had been a great night.

As the car passed through the traffic lights at the intersection of Alfred and Thomas, Simon realized that something was very wrong. The car coming towards him quickly on the passenger side shouldn't be there. He had the green light. What was going on? The last thing he heard was a sickening crunch as the car lurched crazily out of control.

Danny woke early. The voices he had thought he heard in the night, he reasoned, must have been part of a lost dream. He decided that he would go jogging even though on Saturdays he usually stayed in bed and slept. He was feeling better in spite of his crowded dreaming. Pulling on his sneakers his mind returned to the events of the previous night. He hoped Simon wouldn't have been put out by his leaving the party early. Simon was probably glad, Danny concluded, he could have Mandy all to himself.

The morning was cool and crisp and there was a dew over the lawns as Danny jogged along his usual route. He decided to detour over to Simon's. As he turned the corner he saw a police car in the driveway and people standing around in their dressing gowns. Danny slowed, questioning their presence.

"What's wrong?"

A burly police officer left the group and walked over to Danny.

"Do you know a Mrs. Joan Brennan?"

"Yeah—that's Simon's mom."

"Who are you?"

Danny gave his name.

"Her car was involved in a serious accident early this morning. We haven't been able to identify who was driving the car. No one is home here."

Danny felt as if he had been hit. He reeled back. He heard his voice question the officer.

"What happened?"

"A car hit the Brennan's car by going through a red light. Poor kids inside didn't have a chance."

"Are they all right?"

"Do you know who could've been in the car?"

Danny felt like passing out.

"My best mate—Simon Brennan, and probably Amanda Sokolich, his girlfriend."

"Your friend is unconscious but probably will be all right... I'm afraid the girl is dead—killed instantly. There was nothing they could do."

The policeman gave Danny a few moments for the news to sink in. He watched his face for signs of shock.

"Danny," he said slowly, "do you know where the residents of the house are?"

Danny fought to remain in control. If he hadn't left early it could have been him too, he thought. His voice cracked with emotion when he replied to the officer.

"They're at their beach house near Madora Bay, I've been down there plenty of times, and I know where Amanda…lives." With an awful realization, Danny felt the full impact of the irony of the word he had just uttered.

"Yes, we've established her address. Could you come with me in the squad car to Madora Bay? That would save me considerable time."

"If you wouldn't mind running me home first. I'll have to tell my mom."

As the police car pulled up in front of Danny's place, he wanted to ask all sorts of questions, but was scared of knowing the answers and realized it would not be proper anyway. The officer left the motor running.

As the car moved away, Danny sank back into the seat. He felt that he was in the middle of a nightmare. As the car turned onto the highway the early morning sun in the east momentarily dazzled him. The red sky heralded a day that Danny wished was not happening. The white markings on the road racing to meet the car hypnotized him as he sat motionless.

O B I T U A R Y

SOKOLICH,—A.M.
Much loved daughter of Bev and Joe and sister of Ben. Tragically taken. Aged 16 years. May perpetual light shine upon her.

SOKOLICH,—M.
Deepest sympathy Mrs. Sokolich and Ben. I'll never forget you.
Helga.

SOKOLICH,—M.
Goodbye Mandy.
Love Danny.

SOKOLICH,—M.
The Principal and Staff of Cobalt High School extend their sympathy to the family of Mandy on the tragic loss of their daughter and sister.

SALLY

Isaac Asimov

ally was coming down the lake road, so I waved to her and called her by name. I always liked to see Sally. I liked all of them, you understand, but Sally's the prettiest one of the lot. There just isn't any question about it.

She moved a little faster when I waved to her. Nothing undignified. She was never that. She moved just enough faster to show that she was glad to see me, too.

I turned to the man standing beside me. "That's Sally," I said.

He smiled at me and nodded.

Mrs. Hester had brought him in. She said, "This is Mr. Gellhorn, Jake. You remember he sent you the letter asking for an appointment."

That was just talk, really. I have a million things to do around the Farm, and one thing I just can't waste my time on is mail. That's why I have Mrs. Hester around. She lives close by, she's good at attending to foolishness without running to me about it, and most of all she likes Sally and the rest. Some people don't.

"Glad to see you, Mr. Gellhorn," I said.

"Raymond J. Gellhorn," he said, and gave me his hand, which I shook and gave back.

He was a largish fellow, half a head taller than I and wider, too. He was about half my age, thirtyish. He had black hair, plastered down slick, with a part in the middle, and a thin mustache, very neatly trimmed. His jawbones got big under his ears and made him look as if he had a slight case of mumps. On video he'd be a natural to play the villain, so I assumed he was a nice fellow. It goes to show that video can't be wrong all the time.

"I'm Jacob Folkers," I said. "What can I do for you?"

He grinned. It was a big, wide, white-toothed grin. "You can tell me a little about your Farm here, if you don't mind."

I heard Sally coming up behind me and I put out my hand. She slid right into it and the feel of the hard, glossy enamel of her fender was warm in my palm.

"A nice automatobile," said Gellhorn.

That's one way of putting it. Sally was a 2045 convertible

with a Hennis-Carleton positronic motor and an Armat chassis. She had the cleanest, finest lines I've ever seen on any model, bar none. For five years, she'd been my favourite, and I'd put everything into her I could dream up. In all that time, there'd never been a human being behind her wheel.

Not once.

"Sally," I said, patting her gently, "meet Mr. Gellhorn."

Sally's cylinder-purr keyed up a little. I listened carefully for any knocking. Lately, I'd been hearing motor-knock in almost all the cars and changing the gasoline hadn't done a bit of good. Sally was as smooth as her paint job this time, however.

"Do you have names for all your cars?" asked Gellhorn.

He sounded amused, and Mrs. Hester doesn't like people to sound as though they are making fun of the Farm. She said, sharply, "Certainly. The cars have real personalities, don't they, Jake? The sedans are all males and the convertibles are females."

Gellhorn was smiling again. "And do you keep them in separate garages, ma'am?"

Gellhorn said to me, "And now I wonder if I can talk to you alone, Mr. Folkers?"

"That depends," I said. "Are you a reporter?"

"No, sir. I'm a sales agent. Any talk we have is not for publication. I assure you I am interested in strict privacy."

"Let's walk down the road a bit. There's a bench there."

We started down. Mrs. Hester walked away. Sally nudged along after us.

I said, "You don't mind if Sally comes along, do you?"

"Not at all. She can't repeat what we say, can she?" He laughed at his own joke, reached over and rubbed Sally's grille.

Sally raced her motor and Gellhorn's hand drew away quickly.

"She's not used to strangers," I explained.

We sat down on the bench under the big oak tree where we could look across the small lake to the private speedway. It was the warm part of the day and the cars were out in force, at least thirty of them. Even at this distance I could see that Jeremiah was pulling his usual stunt of sneaking up behind some staid older model, then putting on a jerk of speed and yowling past with deliberately squealing brakes. Two weeks before he had crowded old Angus off the asphalt altogether, and I had turned off his motor for two days.

It didn't help, though, I'm afraid, and it looks as though there's nothing to be done about it. Jeremiah is a sports model to begin with and that kind is awfully hot-headed.

"Well, Mr. Gellhorn," I said. "Could you tell me why you want the information?"

But he was just looking around. He said, "This *is* an amazing place, Mr. Folkers."

"I wish you'd call me Jake. Everyone does."

"All right, Jake. How many cars do you have here?"

"Fifty-one. We get one or two new ones every year. One year we got five. We haven't lost one yet. They're all in perfect running order. We even have a '15 model Mat-O-Mot in working order. One of the original automatics. It was the first car here."

Good old Matthew. He stayed in the garage most of the day now, but then he was the grandaddy of all positronic-motored cars. Those were the days when blind war veterans, paraplegics and heads of state were the only ones who drove automatics. But Samson Harridge was my boss, and he was rich enough to be able to get one. I was his chauffeur at the time.

The thought makes me feel old. I can remember when there wasn't an automobile in the world with brains enough to find its own way home. I chauffeured dead lumps of machines that needed a man's hand at their controls every minute. Every year machines like that used to kill tens of thousands of people.

The automatics fixed that. A positronic brain can react much faster than a human one, of course, and it paid people to keep hands off the controls. You got in, punched your destination and let it go its own way.

We take it for granted now, but I remember when the first laws came out forcing the old machines off the highways and limiting travel to automatics. Lord, what a fuss. They called it everything from communism to fascism, but it emptied the highways and stopped the killing, and still more people get around more easily the new way.

Of course, the automatics were ten to a hundred times as expensive as the hand-driven ones, and there weren't many that could afford a private vehicle. The industry specialized in turning out omnibus-automatics. You could always call a company and have one stop at your door in a matter of minutes and take you where you wanted to go. Usually, you had to drive with others who were going your way, but what's wrong with that?

Samson Harridge had a private car though, and I went to him the minute it arrived. The car wasn't Matthew to me then. I didn't know it was going to be the dean of the Farm some day. I only knew it was taking my job away and I hated it.

I said, "You won't be needing me any more, Mr. Harridge?"

He said, "What are you dithering about, Jake? You don't think I'll trust myself to a contraption like that, do you? You stay right at the controls."

I said, "But it works by itself, Mr. Harridge. It scans the road, reacts properly to obstacles, humans, and other cars, and remembers routes to travel."

"So they say. So they say. Just the same, you're sitting right behind the wheel in case anything goes wrong."

Funny how you can get to like a car. In no time I was calling it Matthew and was spending all my time keeping it polished and humming. A positronic brain stays in condition best when it's got control of its chassis at all times, which means it's worth keeping the gas tank filled so that the motor can turn over slowly day and night. After a while, it got so I could tell by the sound of the motor how Matthew felt.

In his own way, Harridge grew fond of Matthew, too. He had no one else to like. He'd divorced or outlived three wives and outlived five children and three grandchildren. So when he died, maybe it wasn't surprising that he had his estate converted into a Farm for Retired Automobiles, with me in charge and Matthew the first member of a distinguished line.

It's turned out to be my life. I never got married. You can't get married and still tend to automatics the way you should.

The newspapers thought it was funny, but after a while they stopped joking about it. Some things you can't joke about. Maybe you've never been able to afford an automatic and maybe you never will, either, but take it from me, you get to love them. They're hard-working and affectionate. It takes a man with no heart to mistreat one or to see one mistreated.

It got so that after a man had an automatic for a while, he would make provisions for having it left to the Farm, if he didn't have an heir he could rely on to give it good care.

I explained that to Gellhorn.

He said, "Fifty one cars! That represents a lot of money."

"Fifty thousand minimum per automatic, original investment," I said. "They're worth more now. I've done things for them."

"It must take a lot of money to keep up the Farm."

"You're right there. The Farm's a non-profit organization, which gives us a break on taxes and, of course, new automatics that come in usually have trust funds attached. Still, costs are always going up. I have to keep the place landscaped; I keep laying down new asphalt and keeping the old in repair; there's gasoline, oil, repairs, and new gadgets. It adds up."

"And you've spent a long time at it."

"I sure have, Mr. Gellhorn. Thirty-three years."

"You don't seem to be getting much out of it yourself."

"I don't? You surprise me, Mr. Gellhorn. I've got Sally and fifty others. Look at her."

I was grinning. I couldn't help it. Sally was so clean, it almost hurt. Some insect must have died on her windshield or one speck of dust too many had landed, so she was going to work. A little tube protruded and spurted Tergosol over the glass. It spread quickly over the silicone surface film and squeejees snapped into place instantly, passing over the windshield and forcing the water into the little channel that led it, dripping, down to the ground. Not a speck of water got onto her glistening apple-green hood.

Squeejee and detergent tube snapped back into place and disappeared.

Gellhorn said, "I never saw an automatic do that."

"I guess not," I said. "I fixed that up specially on our cars. They're clean. They're always scrubbing their glass. They like it. I've even got Sally fixed up with wax jets. She polishes herself every night till you can see your face in any part of her and shave by it. If I can scrape up the money, I'll be putting it on the rest of the girls. Convertibles are very vain."

"I can tell you how to scrape up the money, if that interests you."

"That always does. How?"

"Isn't it obvious, Jake? Any of your cars is worth fifty thousand minimum, you said. I'll bet most of them top six figures."

"So?"

"Ever think of selling a few?"

I shook my head. "You don't realize it, I guess, Mr. Gellhorn, but I can't sell any of these. They belong to the Farm, not to me."

"The money would go to the Farm."

"The incorporation papers of the Farm provide that the cars receive perpetual care. They can't be sold."

"What about the motors, then?"

"I don't understand you."

Gellhorn shifted position and his voice got confidential. "Look here, Jake, let me explain the situation. There's a big market for private automatics if they could only be made cheaply enough. Right?"

"That's no secret."

"And ninety-five percent of the cost is the motor. Right? Now, I know where we can get a supply of bodies. I also know where we can sell automatics at a good price—twenty or thirty thousand for the cheaper models, maybe fifty or sixty for the better ones. All I need are the motors. You see the solution?"

"I don't, Mr. Gellhorn." I did, but I wanted him to say it.

"It's right here. You've got fifty-one of them. You're an

expert automatobile mechanic, Jake. You must be. You could unhook a motor and place it in another car so that no one would know the difference."

"It wouldn't be exactly ethical."

"You wouldn't be harming the cars. You'd be doing them a favour. Use your older cars. Use that old Mat-O-Mot."

"Well, now, wait a while, Mr. Gellhorn. The motors and bodies aren't two separate items. They're a single unit. Those motors are used to their own bodies. They just wouldn't be happy in another car."

"All right, that's a point. That's a very good point, Jake. It would be like taking your mind and putting it in someone else's skull, right? You don't think you would like that?"

"I don't think I would. No."

"But what if I took your mind and put it into the body of a young athlete. What about that, Jake? You're not a youngster anymore. If you had the chance, wouldn't you enjoy being twenty again? That's what I'm offering some of your positronic motors. They'll be put into new '57 bodies. The latest construction."

I laughed. "That doesn't make much sense, Mr. Gellhorn. Some of our cars may be old, but they're well-cared for. Nobody drives them. They're allowed their own way. They're *retired*, Mr. Gellhorn. I wouldn't want a twenty-year old body if it meant I had to dig ditches for the rest of my new life and never have enough to eat…What do you think, Sally?"

Sally's two doors opened and shut with a cushioned slam.

"What's that?" said Gellhorn.

"That's the way Sally laughs."

Gellhorn forced a smile. I guess he thought I was making a bad joke. He said, "Talk sense, Jake. Cars are *made* to be driven. They're probably not happy if you don't drive them."

I said, "Sally hasn't been driven in five years. She looks happy to me."

"I wonder."

He got up and walked toward Sally slowly. "Hi, Sally, how'd you like a drive?"

Sally's motor revved up. She backed away.

"Don't push her, Mr. Gellhorn," I said. "She's liable to be a little skittish."

Two sedans were about a hundred metres up the road. They had stopped. Maybe, in their own way, they were watching. I didn't bother about them. I had my eyes on Sally, and I kept them there.

Gellhorn said, "Steady now, Sally." He lunged out and seized the door handle. It didn't budge, of course.

He said, "It opened a minute ago."

I said, "Automatic lock. She's got a sense of privacy."

He let go, then said, slowly and deliberately, "A car with a sense of privacy shouldn't go around with its top down."

He stepped back three or four paces, then quickly, so quickly I couldn't take a step to stop him, he ran forward and vaulted into the car. He caught Sally completely by surprise, because as he came down, he shut off the ignition before she could lock it in place.

For the first time in five years, Sally's motor was dead.

I think I yelled, but Gellhorn had the switch on "Manual" and locked that in place, too. He kicked the motor into action. Sally was alive again but she had no freedom of action.

He started up the road. The sedans were still there. They turned and drifted away, not very quickly. I suppose it was all a puzzle to them.

One was Giuseppe, from the Milan factories, and the other was Stephen. They were always together. They were both new at the Farm, but they'd been here long enough to know that our cars just didn't have drivers.

Gellhorn went straight on, and when the sedans finally got it through their heads that Sally wasn't going to slow down, that she *couldn't* slow down, it was too late for anything but desperate measures.

They broke for it, one to each side, and Sally raced between them like a streak. Steve crashed through the lakeside fence and rolled to a halt on the grass and mud not fifteen centimetres from the water's edge. Giuseppe bumped along the land side of the road to a shaken halt.

I had Steve back on the highway and was trying to find out what harm, if any, the fence had done him, when Gellhorn came back.

Gellhorn opened Sally's door and stepped out. Leaning back, he shut off the ignition a second time.

"There," he said. "I think I did her a lot of good."

I held my temper. "Why did you dash through the sedans? There was no reason for that."

"I kept expecting them to turn out."

"They did. One went through a fence."

"I'm sorry, Jake," he said. "I thought they'd move more quickly. You know how it is. I've been in lots of buses, but I've only been in a private automatic two or three times in my life, and this is the first time I ever drove one. That just shows you, Jake. It got me, driving one, and I'm pretty hard-boiled. I tell you, we don't have to go more than twenty percent below list price to reach a good market, and it would be ninety per cent profit."

"Which we would split?"

"Fifty-fifty. And I take all the risks, remember."

"All right. I listened to you. Now you listen to me." I raised my voice because I was just too mad to be polite anymore. "When you turn off Sally's motor, you hurt her. How would you like to be kicked unconscious? That's what you do to Sally, when you turn her off."

"You're exaggerating, Jake. The automatobuses get turned off every night."

"Sure, that's why I want none of my boys or girls in your fancy '57 bodies, where I won't know what treatment they'll get. Buses need major repairs in their positronic circuits every couple of years. Old Matthew hasn't had his circuit touched in twenty years. What can you offer him compared with that?"

"Well, you're excited now. Suppose you think over my proposition when you've cooled down and get in touch with me."

"I've thought it over all I want to. If I ever see you again, I'll call the police."

His mouth got hard and ugly. "Just a minute, old-timer."

I said, "Just a minute, you. This is private property and I'm ordering you off."

He shrugged. "Well, then, goodbye."

I said, "Mrs. Hester will see you off the property. Make that goodbye permanent."

But it wasn't permanent. I saw him again two days later. Two and a half days, rather, because it was about noon when I saw him first and a little after midnight when I saw him again.

I sat up in bed when he turned the light on, blinking blindly until I made out what was happening. Once I could see, it didn't take much explaining. In fact, it took none at all. He had a gun in his right fist, the nasty little needle barrel just visible between two fingers. I knew that all he had to do was to increase the pressure of his hand and I would be torn apart.

He said, "Put on your clothes, Jake."

I didn't move. I just watched him.

He said, "Look, Jake, I know the situation. I visited you two days ago, remember. You have no guards on this place, no electrified fences, no warning signals. Nothing."

I said, "I don't need any. Meanwhile there's nothing to stop you from leaving, Mr. Gellhorn. I would if I were you. This place can be very dangerous."

He laughed a little. "It is, for anyone on the wrong side of a fist gun."

"I see it," I said. "I know you've got one."

"Then get a move on. My men are waiting."

"No sir, Mr. Gellhorn. Not unless you tell me what you want, and probably not then."

"I made you a proposition day before yesterday."

"The answer's still no."

"There's more to the proposition now. I've come here with some men and an automatobus. You have your chance to come with me and disconnect twenty-five of the positronic motors. I don't care which twenty-five you choose. We'll load them on the bus and take them away. Once they're disposed of, I'll see to it that you get your fair share of the money."

"I have your word on that, I suppose."

He didn't act as if he thought I was being sarcastic. He said, "You have."

I said, "No."

"If you insist on saying no, we'll go about it in our own way. I'll disconnect the motors myself, only I'll disconnect all fifty-one. Every one of them."

"It isn't easy to disconnect positronic motors, Mr. Gellhorn. Are you a robotics expert? Even if you are, you know, these motors have been modified by me."

"I know that, Jake. And to be truthful, I'm not an expert. I may ruin quite a few motors trying to get them out. That's why I'll have to work over all fifty-one if you don't cooperate. You see, I may only end up with twenty-five when I'm through. The first few I'll tackle will probably suffer the most. 'Till I get the hang of it, you see. And if I do it myself, I think I'll put Sally first in line."

I said, "I can't believe you're serious, Mr. Gellhorn."

He said, "I'm serious, Jake." He let it all dribble in. "If you want to help, you can keep Sally. Otherwise, she's liable to be hurt very badly. Sorry."

I said, "I'll come with you, but I'll give you one more warning. You'll be in trouble, Mr. Gellhorn."

He thought that was very funny. He was laughing very quietly as we went down the stairs together.

There was an automatobus waiting outside the driveway to the garage apartments. The shadows of three men waited beside it, and their flash beams went on as we approached.

Gellhorn said in a low voice, "I've got the old fellow. Come on. Move the truck up the drive and let's get started."

One of the others leaned in and punched the proper instructions on the control panel. We moved up the driveway with the bus following submissively.

"It won't go inside the garage," I said. "The door won't take it. We don't have buses here. Only private cars."

"All right," said Gellhorn. "Pull it over onto the grass and keep it out of sight."

I could hear the thrumming of the cars when we were still ten metres from the garage.

Usually they quieted down if I entered the garage. This time they didn't. I think they knew that strangers were about, and once the faces of Gellhorn and the others were visible they got noisier. Each motor was a warm rumble, and each motor was knocking irregularly until the place rattled.

The lights went up automatically as we stepped inside. Gellhorn didn't seem bothered by the car noise, but the three men with him looked surprised and uncomfortable. They had the look of the hired thug about them, a look that was not compounded of physical features so much as of a certain wariness of eye and hang-dogness of face. I knew the type and I wasn't worried.

One of them said, "Damn it, they're burning gas."

"My cars always do," I replied stiffly.

"Not tonight," said Gellhorn. "Turn them off."

"It's not that easy, Mr. Gellhorn," I said.

"Get started!" he said.

I stood there. He had his fist gun pointed at me steadily. I said, "I told you, Mr. Gellhorn, that my cars have been well-treated while they've been at the Farm. They're used to being treated that way, and they resent anything else."

"You have one minute. Lecture me some other time."

"I'm trying to explain something. I'm trying to explain that my cars can understand what I say to them. A positronic motor will learn to do that with time and patience. My cars have learned. Sally understood your proposition two days ago. You'll remember she laughed when I asked her opinion. She also knows what you did to her and so do the two sedans you scattered. And the rest know what to do about trespassers in general."

"Look, you crazy old fool—"

"All I have to say is—" I raised my voice. "Get them!"

One of the men turned pasty and yelled, but his voice was drowned completely in the sound of fifty-one horns turned loose at once. They held their notes, and within the four walls of the garage the echoes rose to a wild, metallic call. Two cars rolled forward, not hurriedly, but with no possible mistake as to their target. Two cars fell in line behind the first two. All the cars were stirring in their separate stalls.

The thugs stared, then backed.

I shouted, "Don't get up against a wall."

Apparently, they had that instinctive thought themselves. They rushed madly for the door of the garage.

At the door, one of Gellhorn's men turned and brought up a fist gun of his own. The needle pellet tore a thin, blue flash toward the first car. The car was Giuseppe.

A thin line of paint peeled up on Giuseppe's hood, and the right half of his windshield crazed and splintered but did not break through.

The men were out the door, running, and two by two the cars crunched out after them into the night, their horns calling the charge.

I kept my hand on Gellhorn's elbow, but I don't think he could have moved in any case. His lips were trembling.

I said, "That's why I don't need electrified fences or guards. My property protects itself."

Gellhorn's eyes swivelled back and forth in fascination as, pair by pair, they whizzed by. He said, "They're killers!"

"Don't be silly. They won't kill your men."

"They're killers!"

"They'll just give your men a lesson. My cars have been specially trained for cross-country pursuit for just such an occasion; I think what your men will get will be worse than an outright quick kill. Have you ever been chased by an automatobile?"

Gellhorn didn't answer.

I went on. I didn't want him to miss a thing. "They'll be shadows going no faster than your men, chasing them here, blocking them there, blaring at them, dashing at them, missing with a screech of brake and a thunder of motor. They'll keep it up till your men drop, out of breath and half-dead, waiting for the wheels to crunch over their breaking bones. The cars won't do that. They'll turn away. You can bet, though, that your men will never return here in their lives. Not for all the money you or ten like you could give them. Listen—"

I tightened my hold on his elbow. He strained to hear.

I said, "Don't you hear car doors slamming?"

It was faint and distant, but unmistakable.

I said, "They're laughing. They're enjoying themselves."

His face crumpled with rage. He lifted his hand. He was still holding his fist gun.

I said, "I wouldn't. One automatocar is still with us."

I don't think he had noticed Sally till then. She had moved up so quietly. Though her right front fender nearly touched me, I couldn't hear her motor. She might have been holding her breath.

Gellhorn yelled.

I said, "She won't touch you, as long as I'm with you. But if you kill me.... You know, Sally doesn't like you."

Gellhorn turned the gun in Sally's direction.

"Her motor is shielded," I said, "and before you could ever squeeze the gun a second time she would be on top of you."

"All right, then," he yelled, and suddenly my arm was bent

behind my back and twisted so I could hardly stand. He held me between Sally and himself, and his pressure didn't let up. "Back out with me and don't try to break loose, old-timer, or I'll tear your arm out of its socket."

I had to move. Sally nudged along with us, worried, uncertain what to do. I tried to say something to her and couldn't. I could only clench my teeth and moan.

Gellhorn's automatobus was still standing outside the garage. I was forced in. Gellhorn jumped in after me, locking the doors behind him.

He said, "All right, now. We'll talk sense."

I was rubbing my arm, trying to get life back into it, and even as I did I was automatically and without any conscious effort studying the control board of the bus.

I said, "This is a rebuilt job."

"So?" he said caustically. "It's a sample of my work. I picked up a discarded chassis, found a brain I could use and spliced me a private bus. What of it?"

I tore at the repair panel, forcing it aside.

He said, "What the hell. Get away from that." The side of his palm came down numbingly on my left shoulder.

I struggled with him. "I don't want to do this bus any harm. What kind of a person do you think I am? I just want to take a look at some of the motor connections."

It didn't take much of a look. I was boiling when I turned to him. I said, "You're a rotten person. You had no right installing this motor yourself. Why didn't you get a robotics man?"

He said, "Do I look crazy?"

"Even if it was a stolen motor, you had no right to treat it so. I wouldn't treat a man the way you treated that motor. Solder, tape, and pinch clamps! It's brutal!"

"It works, doesn't it?"

"Sure it works, but it must be hell for the bus. You could live with migraine headaches and acute arthritis, but it wouldn't be much of a life. This car is *suffering*."

"Shut up!" For a moment he glanced out the window at

Sally, who had rolled up as close to the bus as she could. He made sure the doors and windows were locked.

He said, "We're getting out of here now, before the other cars come back. We'll stay away."

"How will that help you?"

"Your cars will run out of gas someday, won't they? You haven't got them fixed up so they can tank up on their own, have you? We'll come back and finish the job."

"They'll be looking for me," I said. "Mrs. Hester will call the police."

He was past reasoning with. He just punched the bus in gear. It lurched forward. Sally followed.

He giggled. "What can she do if you're here with me?"

Sally seemed to realize that, too. She picked up speed, passed us and was gone. Gellhorn opened the window next to him and spat through the opening.

The bus lumbered on over the dark road, its motor rattling unevenly. Gellhorn dimmed the periphery light until the phosphorescent green stripe down the middle of the highway, sparkling in the moonlight, was all that kept us out of the trees. There was virtually no traffic. Two cars passed ours, going the other way, and there was none at all on our side of the highway, either before or behind.

I heard the door-slamming first. Quick and sharp in the silence, first on the right and then on the left. Gellhorn's hands quivered as he punched savagely for increased speed. A beam of light shot out from among a scrub of trees, blinding us. Another beam plunged at us from behind the guard rails on the other side. At a crossover, three hundred fifty metres ahead, there was a sque-e-e-e as a car darted across our path.

"Sally went for the rest," I said. "I think you're surrounded."

"So what? What can they do?"

He hunched over the controls, peering through the windshield.

"And don't *you* try anything old-timer," he muttered.

I couldn't. I was bone-weary; my left arm was on fire. The motor sounds gathered and grew closer. I could hear the motors missing in odd patterns; suddenly it seemed to me that my cars were speaking to one another.

A medley of horns came from behind. I turned and Gellhorn looked quickly into the rearview mirror. A dozen cars were following in both lanes.

Gellhorn yelled and laughed madly.

I cried, "Stop! Stop the car!"

Because not half a kilometre ahead, plainly visible in the light beams of two sedans on the roadside was Sally, her trim body plunked square across the road. Two cars shot into the opposite lane to our left, keeping perfect time with us and preventing Gellhorn from turning out.

But he had no intention of turning out. He put his finger on the full-speed-ahead button and kept it there.

He said, "There'll be no bluffing here. This bus outweighs her five to one, old-timer, and we'll just push her off the road like a dead kitten."

I knew he could. The bus was on manual and his finger was on the button. I knew he would.

I lowered the window, and stuck my head out. "Sally," I screamed. "Get out of the way. *Sally!*"

It was drowned out in the agonized squeal of maltreated brakebands. I felt myself thrown forward and heard Gellhorn's breath puff out of his body.

I said, "What happened?" It was a foolish question. We had stopped. That was what had happened. Sally and the bus were one and a half metres apart. With five times her weight tearing down on her, she had not budged. The guts of her.

Gellhorn yanked at the Manual toggle switch. "It's got to," he kept muttering. "It's got to."

I said, "Not the way you hooked up the motor, expert. Any of the circuits could cross over."

He looked at me with a tearing anger and growled deep in his throat. His hair was matted over his forehead. He lifted his fist gun.

"That's all the advice out of you there'll ever be, old-timer."

And I knew the needle gun was about to fire.

I pressed back against the bus door, watching the fist come up, and when the door opened I went over backward and out, hitting the ground with a thud. I heard the door slam closed again.

I got to my knees and looked up in time to see Gellhorn struggle uselessly with the closing window, then aim his fist-gun quickly through the glass. He never fired. The bus got under way with a tremendous roar, and Gellhorn lurched backward.

Sally wasn't in the way any longer, and I watched the bus's rear lights flicker away down the highway.

I was exhausted. I sat down right there, right on the highway, and put my head down in my crossed arms, trying to catch my breath.

I heard a car stop gently at my side. When I looked up, it was Sally. Slowly—lovingly, you might say—her front door opened.

No one had driven Sally for five years—except Gellhorn, of course—and I knew how valuable such freedom was to a car. I appreciated the gesture, but I said, "Thanks, Sally, but I'll take one of the newer cars."

I got up and turned away, but skillfully and neatly as a pirouette, she wheeled before me again. I couldn't hurt her feelings. I got in. Her front seat had the fine, fresh scent of an automobile that kept itself spotlessly clean. I lay down across it, thankfully, and with even, silent, and rapid efficiency, my boys and girls brought me home.

Mrs. Hester brought me the copy of the radio transcript the next evening with great excitement.

"It's Mr. Gellhorn," she said. "The man who came to see you."

"What about him?"

I dreaded her answer.

"They found him dead," she said. "Imagine that. Just lying dead in a ditch."

"It might be a stranger altogether," I mumbled.

"Raymond J. Gellhorn," she said, sharply. "There can't be two, can there? The description fits, too. Lord, what a way to die! They found tire marks on his arms and body. Imagine! I'm glad it turned out to be a bus; otherwise they might have come poking around here."

"Did it happen near here?" I asked, anxiously.

"No...Near Cooksville. But, goodness, read about it yourself if you—What happened to Giuseppe?"

I welcomed the diversion. Giuseppe was waiting patiently for me to complete the repaint job. His windshield had been replaced.

After she left, I snatched up the transcript. There was no doubt about it. The doctor reported he had been running and was in a state of totally spent exhaustion. I wondered for how many kilometres the bus had played with him before the final lunge. The transcript had no notion of anything like that, of course.

They had located the bus and identified it by the tire tracks. The police had it and were trying to trace its ownership.

There was an editorial in the transcript about it. It had been the first traffic fatality in the state for that year, and the paper warned strenuously against manual driving after night.

There was no mention of Gellhorn's three thugs and for that, at least, I was grateful. None of our cars had been seduced by the pleasure of the chase into killing.

That was all. I let the paper drop. Gellhorn had been a criminal. His treatment of the bus had been brutal. There was not question in my mind he deserved death. But still I felt a bit queasy over the manner of it.

A month has passed now and I can't get it out of my mind. My cars talk to one another. I have no doubt about it anymore. It's as though they've gained confidence; as though they're not bothering to keep it secret anymore. Their engines rattle and knock continuously.

And they don't talk among themselves only. They talk to the cars and buses that come into the Farm on business. How long have they been doing that?

They must be understood, too. Gellhorn's bus understood them for all it hadn't been on the grounds more than an hour. I can close my eyes and bring back that dash along the highway, with our cars flanking the bus on either side, clacking their motors at it until it understood, stopped, let me out, and ran off with Gellhorn.

Did my cars tell him to kill Gellhorn? Or was that his idea?

Can cars have such ideas? The motor designers say no. But they mean under ordinary conditions. Have they foreseen *everything*?

Cars get ill-used, you know.

Some of them enter the Farm and observe. They get told things. They find out that cars exist whose motors are never stopped, whom no one ever drives, whose every need is supplied.

Then maybe they go out and tell others. Maybe the word is spreading quickly. Maybe they're going to think that the Farm way should be the way all over the world. They don't understand. You couldn't expect them to understand about legacies and the whims of rich men.

There are millions of automobiles on Earth, tens of millions. If the thought gets rooted in them that they're slaves; that they should do something about it...If they begin to think the way Gellhorn's bus did....

Maybe it won't be until after my time. And then they'll have to keep a few of us to take care of them, won't they? They wouldn't kill us all.

Or maybe they would. Maybe they wouldn't understand about how someone would have to care for them. Maybe they won't wait.

Every morning I wake up and think, Maybe today....

I don't get as much pleasure out of my cars as I used to. Lately, I notice that I'm even beginning to avoid Sally.

The phrase "home sweet home" is not always true. You don't always understand your parents, and they don't always understand you. But even with the ups and downs, you probably still agree... "Home is where the heart is."

BE IT EVER SO RENT FREE

Bill Cosby

Your reward for being a parent will be that some day your daughter will come home to you and stay, perhaps at the age of forty-three. More and more children these days are moving back home a decade or two after they have stopped being children because the schools have been making the mistake of teaching Robert Frost, who said, "Home is the place where, when you go there, they have to take you in." Why don't they teach *You Can't Go Home Again* instead?

I recently met a man and woman who had been married for fifty years and they told me a story with enough horror for Brian De Palma. Their forty-six-year-old son had just moved back in with them, bringing his two kids, one who was twenty-three and one who was twenty-two. All three of them were out of work.

"And that," I told my wife, "is why there is death."

Who wants to be seven hundred years old and look out the window and see your six-hundred-year-old son coming home to live with you? Bringing his two four-hundred-year-old kids.

I have five children and I love them as much as a father possibly could, but I confess that I have an extra bit of appreciation for my nine-year-old.

"Why do you love her so much?" the other kids keep asking me.

And I reply, "Because she's the last one. And I never thought that would occur. If I'm still alive when she leaves at eighteen, my golden age can finally begin."

I find there is almost music to whatever this child does, for, whatever she does, it's the last time I will have to be a witness to that event. She could set the house on fire and I would say, "Well, that's the last time the house will burn down."

She is as bad as the others, this nine-year-old; in fact, she learns faster how to be bad; but I still look at her with that extra bit of appreciation and I also smile a lot because she is the final one.

I sympathize with the older ones for not understanding. They are perplexed because things they did that annoyed me are now adorable when done by the nine-year-old. When the older ones took pages from a script I was writing and used them for origami, I was annoyed; but when the last one does it, I feel good all over.

After their last one has grown up, many fathers think that the golden age of solitude has arrived, but it turns out to be fool's gold, for their married children have this habit of getting divorced; and then they drop off the children at your house while they go to find another spouse.

And sometimes it is not only the children but animals, too.

"Dad, I wonder if you could watch our horse while we're away."

"Well, what if your mother and I decide to go someplace?" you say.

"You people are *old*. You don't *go* anywhere."

The only reason we had children was to give them love and wisdom and then freedom. But it's a package deal: the first two have to lead to the third. Freedom—the thing so precious to Thomas Jefferson. He didn't want *his* kids coming back either, especially because he had *six* of them.

In spite of all the scientific knowledge to date, I have to say that the human animal cannot be the most intelligent one on earth because he is the only one who allows his offspring to come back home. Look at anything that gives birth: eventually it will run and hide. After a while, even a mother elephant will run away from its child and hide. And when you consider how hard it is for a mother elephant to hide, you can appreciate the depth of her motivation.

AMANDA AND THE WOUNDED BIRDS

Colby Rodowsky

I t's not that my mother doesn't understand, because she does. In fact, she understands so well, and so much, and so single-mindedly that half the time she goes around with a glazed look in her eyes and forgets to get her hair cut, and go to the dentist and that we're almost out of toilet paper or tuna fish.

She makes her living understanding, which may make more sense when I tell you that my mother is Dr. Emma Hart. Now, if that doesn't help, then probably, like me until my consciousness was raised, you've always thought of radio as the place to hear the Top 40 or sometimes the weather report when you're heading for the shore on a summer Friday afternoon. But just try twiddling the dial and you'll find her, way over to the left on the band, next to the country and western station.

Maybe what I should do is go back a little and explain. You see, my mother is a psychotherapist, which means that she counsels people and tries to help them find ways of dealing with their problems. She's also a widow. My father died when I was a baby and sometimes I try to imagine what it must have been like for her, taking care of a baby alone and trying to establish a practice all at the same time. One thing I'm sure of is that knowing Mom, she handled it gracefully, and stoically, and with that funny way she has of biting her lower lip so that for all her hanging-in-there attitude she still looks like a ten-year-old kid— the kind you want to do something for because she's not always whining or sniffling. I guess you'd have to say that as much as possible my mother is in charge of her own life, which is the way she tries to get the people who call in to her on the radio to be.

The way the radio program got started was that several years ago the producer was looking for something to put on in the late afternoon when people were mostly fixing dinner or driving car pool or just sitting with their feet up. It wasn't exactly prime time. Then he remembered how he'd heard Mom speak at a dinner once and had thought at the time that putting someone like her on radio would be a real public service. Besides, the ratings couldn't be any lower than they had been for the Handy Home Fixit show he'd had on before. Anyway, he tracked her down, arranged for a test, and then Mom was on the air.

I never will forget that first show. I mean, there was my mother's voice coming out of our kitchen radio, sounding slightly frantic and giving those first callers more than they bargained for: I guess she was afraid if she let them off the line there wouldn't *be* any more. That day even the producer called with a question. And the boy in the studio who went for coffee. But Mom hung in there, and calls continued to come in, and then they started backing up, and it wasn't long before people opened by saying, "I didn't think I'd *ever* get through to you." After only a month on the air the Emma Hart show went from one hour to two; and the way I figured it, a lot of people were eating dinner later than they ever had before. Including us.

Mom really cared about the people who telephoned her, and almost right from the beginning she was calling them her "wounded birds." Not on the air, of course, and *never* to anyone but me. I got used to her looking up in the middle of dinner or from watching the late news on TV and saying, "I hope my wounded bird with the abusive husband will get herself into counseling," or "The wounded bird with those children who walk all over her had better learn to assert herself before it's too late." And *I sure* learned not to joke around: once I referred to one of her callers as a fractured canary and almost started World War III.

Not long after this, things really started to happen. First, Mom's show was moved to a better time slot. Then it was syndicated, so that she wasn't just on the air here but in a bunch of other cities, too. The way "Doonesbury" and "Dick Tracy" are in a bunch of newspapers. Now, I have to say that for the most part my mother's pretty cool about things, but the day she found out that the Emma Hart show was being syndicated she just about flipped. She called me from the studio and told me to meet her at the Terrace Garden for dinner, to be sure and get spiffed up because we were going all out.

During dinner Mom spent a lot of time staring into the candlelight and smiling to herself. Finally she said, "Just think of all those people who'll be listening now." And let me tell you, I *was* thinking about them, and it worried me a lot. I mean the way I saw it, there were going to be even more problems: more victims who were downtrodden or misunderstood. More stories about people who had been abused or who had kids on drugs or dropping out, or ne'er-do-well relatives moving in. But when I tried to say that, Mom was suddenly all attention. "Don't be silly, Amanda. It's the same amount of time and the same number of calls—you'll hardly notice any difference. Only now I'll have wounded birds in Phoenix and Pittsburgh and Philadelphia."

In one way she was right: the show sounded pretty much the same. (Except that *I* found out that when your husband/lover/friend walks out on you it hurts as much in Peoria as it does in Perth Amboy.)

In another way she was wrong: she was busier than she had ever been before, what with travelling and lecturing and doing guest shows from other cities. For a while there, it was as if I was spending as much time at my best friend Terri's as I was at my own house. Then eventually Mom decided I could stay at our place when she had to be out of town, as long as Terri stayed there with me, which wasn't as good or as bad as it sounds, because Terri lives right across the street and her mother has X-ray eyes. I mean we can hardly manage to reach for our favourite breakfast of Twinkies and Oreo ice cream with an orange juice chaser before her mother is on the telephone telling us to eat cornflakes instead—and to wash the dishes.

Sometimes I felt that life was nothing but a revolving door: Mom going out while I was coming in. I know there are some kids who would've thought I was lucky, but the thing about my mother is that she's okay. And I wanted to see more of her. Besides that, I needed to talk to her. I don't know why, but all of a sudden it seemed that things were piling up around me. No major crises, you understand. Nothing that would exactly stop traffic.

I'll give you an example.

Take my friend Terri. I have a terrible feeling that she has a secret crush on my boyfriend Josh. If she does, it would be a disaster, because how could we really be friends anymore? But then again how could Terri and I *not* be friends? I'm not sure *why* I think this, unless it's because she gets quiet and acts bored when I talk about him a lot—the way you do when you don't want to let on about liking someone. I mean she couldn't *really* be bored. Could she?

Then there's Miss Spellman, my English teacher, who has this really atrocious breath and is forever leaning into people as she reads poetry in class. Imagine somebody breathing garbage fumes on you as she recites Emily Dickinson. If something doesn't happen soon I may never like poetry again.

Now, maybe these aren't world problems, any more than the incident with the guidance counselor was, but it bugged me all the same. Our school has an obsession about students getting into *good* colleges a.s.a.p. and knowing what they want to do with the rest of their lives (Terri and I call it the life-packaging syndrome). Anyway, this particular day I was coming out of gym on my way to study hall when Mr. Burnside, the guidance counselor, stopped me and started asking me all this stuff, like what my career goals were and had I decided what I wanted to major in in college.

What I said (only politer than it sounds here) was that how did I know what I wanted to major in when I didn't even know where I wanted to *go* to college. Mr. Burnside got a wild look in his eyes and started opening and closing his mouth so that all I could see was a shiny strand of spit running between his top and bottom teeth while he lectured me on how I was going about this whole college thing the wrong way. He said I should come into the guidance office someday and let him feed me into the computer—well, not me exactly, but stuff like my grades, extra curricular activities, and whether or not I needed financial aid.

"And what does your mother say?" he asked as he rooted in his pocket for a late pass to get me into study hall. "You'll certainly have it easier than anybody else in your class, or the school either for that matter—living with Dr. Emma Hart." He laughed that horselaugh of his and slapped me on the back. "She'll get right to the *Hart* of it." Another laugh. "Anybody else would have to call her on the telephone." His laughter seemed to follow me all the way to study hall. I even heard it bouncing around in my head as I settled down to do my Spanish.

"Anybody else would have to call her on the telephone," he had said.

Why not? I thought as I was walking home from school.

Why not? I asked myself when Josh and I were eating popcorn and playing Scrabble on the living room floor that night.

And pretty soon *why not?* changed to *when?* The answer to that one was easy enough though, because spring vacation was only a week and a half away and that would give me the perfect opportunity.

The funny thing was that once I'd decided to do it, I never worried about getting through. Maybe that was because I'd heard Mom say plenty of times that they always liked it when kids called into the show, and I guess I figured that unless everybody on spring vacation decided to call the Dr. Emma Hart Show, I wouldn't have any trouble. Besides, I practiced in the shower making my voice huskier than usual and just a little breathless, hoping that it would sound sincere and make an impression on Jordan, the guy who screens the calls and tries for just the right balance of men, women, and kids, with not too much emphasis on busted romances as opposed to anxiety attacks.

The next funny thing was that once I'd made up my mind to call Dr. Emma Hart, I began to feel like a wounded bird myself, and I was suddenly awfully glad that she cared about them the way she did. I had a little trouble deciding what I wanted to ask her on the show, and even before I could make up my mind I began to think of other things that bothered me too. Not problems, but stuff I'd like to talk over with Mom. Like Vietnam, for example. I'd watched *Apocalypse Now* on TV and there were a lot of things I didn't understand. And what about the sixties?—was Mom ever involved in sit-ins or walkouts or any of that? I somehow doubted it, but it would be important to know for sure. Finally it came to me: what I wanted to ask Dr. Hart about was not being able to talk to Mom because there she was all wrapped up with her wounded birds. Only the whole thing got confusing, one being the other and all.

Anyway, I did it. I put the call in just before eleven on the Monday morning of spring vacation and almost chickened out when Jordan answered. I had met him a couple of times down at the studio, and I could almost see him now, looking like some kind of an intense juggler who is trying to keep everything going at once. I heard my voice, as if it were coming from somewhere far away, giving my name as Claire (it's my middle name) and outlining my problem. When I got finished, Jordan said that he was putting me on hold and not to go away, that Dr. Hart would be with me shortly.

And all of a sudden she was. I mean, there I was talking to my own mother and telling her how I couldn't talk to my mother, and how the things I wanted to talk to her about weren't actually big deals anyway, but still—

Dr. Hart let me go on for a while and then she broke in and said that it was important for me to know that my concerns were as real as anybody else's and it sounded as if my mother and I had a pretty good relationship that had just gotten a little off the track and what I had to do was be really up-front with her and let her know how I felt. Then she suggested that I make a date with my mother for lunch so that I could tell her (Mom) exactly what I'd told her (Dr. Emma Hart), and that I should be sure to call back and let her know how it worked out.

After that I said, "OK," and "Thank you." Then I hung up.

The only trouble was that as soon as Mom got home that day I knew it wasn't going to work.

She was sort of coming unglued. It had been a bad day, she told me. One of her private patients was in the midst of a crisis; the producer of the show was having a fight with his wife and wanted to tell Mom all about it. She had a dinner speech to give Saturday night and didn't have a thought about what to say, and my uncle Alex had called from Scranton to ask Mom to try to talk some sense into his teenage son, who was driving them all crazy.

Then she looked at me and said, "Thank heavens you've got it all together."

Talk about guilt. Right away I knew I was going to break rule number one: I wasn't going to be able to be up-front.

The thing was, I knew I couldn't take what was already one rotten week for Mom and dump all my problems (which seemed to be getting bigger by the minute) on her. Even though I felt like I was going to explode.

By Friday I knew I needed another talk with Dr. Hart. After all, she'd said to call back, hadn't she?

Getting through Jordan was even easier the second time. All I had to say was that I'd spoken to Dr. Hart earlier in the week and that she'd said to let her know what happened.

"Oh, good, a success story," Jordan said right away, jumping to conclusions. I guess he knew what kind of a week it had been too. "Hold on; Dr. Hart will be with you soon," he said.

And there was Dr. Emma Hart again. And suddenly there *I* was, unloading about how what she had suggested wasn't going to work.

"Why not?" she wanted to know. "Did you try?"

"Yes—no," I said. Then I was going on again, all about Bad-Breath Spellman, the guidance counselor, and how maybe my best friend had a thing for my boyfriend. She kept steering me back to the subject of my mother and why I hadn't arranged to have lunch with her.

I said that my mother had had a bad week. That she was swamped, preoccupied, distracted, and running behind. And then it happened. I mean, I heard the words sliding off my lips and couldn't stop them. I said, "The thing about my mother is that she has all these wounded birds who have really important problems and they take all the time she has."

A silence ballooned up between us and was so loud I

couldn't hear anything else—and if you know anything about radio, you know that the worst thing that can happen is silence. It lasted forever, and while it was going on I gave serious thought to running away from home, or at least hanging up.

When Mom finally spoke, her voice sounded choked, as if she had swallowed a gumball.

"We've been talking to Claire this morning, who is really Amanda," she said. "And one of the things we talk a lot about on this show is saying what you have to say—even if that's not always easy. Are you still there, Amanda?"

"Yes," I squeaked.

"If I know Amanda," my mother went on, "she would rather have run away, or hung up, but instead she did something harder. She hung on."

I gulped.

"Amanda is my daughter, and it seems we have some things to talk about, so what I'm going to do is to ask my assistant to make a reservation for lunch at the Terrace Garden." Then it sounded as though Mom had moved closer to the microphone and was speaking just to me. "If you hurry, Amanda, I'll meet you at 1:30. So we can talk."

And we did: about Bad-Breath Spellman, and Terri, and how it's okay not to know what I want to do with the rest of my life.

We talked about saving the whales, and our two weeks at the shore this summer, and how some day we're going to Ireland. About books and movies and the time in fourth grade when I got the chicken pox and Mom caught them from me.

And we talked about how we had missed talking to each other and what we could do about it.

We ate lunch slowly, and took ages deciding on dessert, and ages more eating it.

We sat there all afternoon, until the light streaking in the windows changed from yellow to a deep, burning gold and the busboys started setting the tables for dinner.

PLAYING GOD

O u i ∂ a   S e b e ∂ t y e n

H e was almost to the river, walking fast, when he saw Laurel on her bicycle, racing to catch him. In a space between the gusts of raw March wind she yelled, "Josh, wait up, or I'll break your legs."

So he wasn't going to get away without saying goodbye after all.

Laurel came puffing up, fierce and wind-whipped. He braced himself as she stared at the duffel bag he'd taken from his folks' closet and stuffed with all the clothes and things he thought he'd need.

"You're doing it," she said. The pain that came into her eyes hurt him, too. "Why? Without telling me? I thought we were friends! If I hadn't seen you sneaking through the alley—"

We *are* friends, he wanted to assure her. Best friends. The best. But he said, walking on, "So? One more thing I didn't do right today." Suddenly it came pouring out. "At breakfast they jumped down my throat about my grades. Then they got started on why can't I grow up and shape up and do my part now with him out of work. Boy. I didn't get him laid off."

"But it's a hard time for them, Josh.'

"Not for her. She's tickled pink. All this schooling's going to get her back into that *career* she gave up when I came along." It seemed vital to stay cold and angry. Even with Laurel. Especially with Laurel, because she knew what he really was. "So I figured I've been enough trouble—I might as well get on out there and do something with my life." He stared at the distant river waiting to be crossed.

"It's dumb," Laurel said, with the directness they had never been afraid to use with each other. "They'll just haul you back. Parents aren't perfect. You're feeling sorry for yourself." She stopped in the road, trying to make him turn around, rethink. But he kept walking. "Please, Josh," she said behind him. "Don't do it."

"*You're* leaving," he said.

"But not until school's out. And I wouldn't be, if we didn't have to move out to the Coast."

"But you are," he said. It wasn't her fault, he knew. She couldn't make her own choices. But he could. "Maybe I'll see you in sunny Cal."

"How'll you live, without money?" she asked into the wind. "Josh? How'll you eat? It scares me."

He turned around. She was outlined against the far-off knob of land called Throne of Kings, where they had sat one day in dusty autumn grass, growing quieter and quieter until their faces turned and their mouths touched in a kiss as intent and sunstruck as the silent hawks gliding over them.

His feet kept moving him backward. "Hey, just don't worry about me," he called. "Nobody else does. Okay?" She didn't answer, but her eyelids blinked fast. He relented. "Would you come as far as the bridge with me?"

She shook her head. "I have to get back to the library. I'm supposed to be helping with the party right now."

Hearing her say she should be getting punch and cookies ready for some stumpy old lady who wrote bad poetry, at the moment he was running away, gave him the new rush of anger he needed to turn around and march out of her life.

The river sprawled ahead of him, more sand than water. There was an eeriness in what he was doing: leaving someone he cared so much about without ending it right. He wished she'd run after him. But what could she say?

When he got to the bridge he looked back, expecting to see her pedalling away, but she stood in the road, her hair blowing across her funny freckled face.

The long bridge turned his footsteps hollow as he started across. He had planned to wait for the bus at the crossroad a kilometre or so farther on. Between wind gusts he found himself straining to hear the hum of traffic. But the only sound was closer, a small lonesome squeak like a bird he didn't recognize, or something grating under the bridge.

When would they notice he'd left home? he wondered. Maybe they wouldn't even miss him.

Near the end of the bridge the sound got louder. He scanned the sky and the flat brown horizon. Then he leaned over the bridge rail and looked down into a cardboard box on the sand at the water's edge. A jumble of yips and squeals came from something dark squirming inside it.

He felt his muscles clamp into knots. He had to catch a bus. He was this far. He had to straighten up and walk on past whatever was down there crying for help. But he couldn't.

He glanced at Laurel. She hadn't moved. He went to the far end of the bridge and climbed down through the weeds. The box twitched as he bent warily and looked in.

Puppies. Five of them, no bigger than fuzzy mittens, crawling in their prison.

Josh drew a weary sigh and squatted to touch them. They went silent, rooting hungrily against his hands. He lifted up a soft black puppy with eyes that melted a hole in his heart, and dropped it back into the pile. "No," he warned them. "I can't do anything, you guys. No."

Their little claws grated on the high sides of the box as they struggled to reach him. He saw Laurel hanging over the bridge rail. "What's down there, Josh?" she called.

"Five puppies," he called back.

She came scrambling down. Her eyes were blazing. "What kind of gutless wonder would throw them into the river! Oh, look at them." She gathered two against her cheeks.

"Maybe somebody couldn't take care of them," he said, trying to be fair. But it wasn't fair. He flicked his hands angrily, staying aloof. "Didn't want to be bothered. So, plop, off the bridge."

"But it's cruel," she said. "It's sad. Like back in early times, in the book Miss Rainey gave you, remember? When people left the defective babies on a mountain so if the gods wanted them saved they could do a miracle." Suddenly she handed him a puppy. "And guess what—along came good old Josh."

"No," he said. "Dang—I've got a bus to catch!" He dropped the puppy into the heap, as trapped as it was. "Why me? What'll I do with the dumb things?"

"You said you've always wanted a dog. You just got five of your wishes." She looked at his eyes and stopped trying to make him smile. "Take them back into town and find them homes. There'll be another bus. If you still..."

He followed her gaze down the road he should be striding along, and turned helplessly to the box. "Want a nice puppy?"

"Oh, I do. But my mom's deathly allergic. And when we move I couldn't take it—we'll be renting until we find a house."

She nudged him up onto the bridge. "Stand in front of the supermarket, Josh. Won't you? Somebody'll take them. Look, I've got to get back, or I'll get canned."

She went to her bike, but her worried eyes kept studying him. He could feel the box pressing against the folded lump of bus ticket money in his pocket. What did she want? Why should he be the one to care, when nobody else did?

"Do you think they'd fall out of my basket if I tried to carry them?" she asked.

"You just worry about getting on back," he said. Her face fell. It touched him to see how hard she was trying to keep this from being goodbye. He shrugged, defeated. "They're not all that heavy. But you could carry the duffel."

Most of the shoppers glanced into his box and went on past to buy their groceries. A few paused. The children stopped and stayed, cuddling puppies until they were dragged away by their parents.

He felt stupid. He resented what those helpless crawling blobs in the box had done to his plans, and was still angry at the person who had left them by the edge of the river. And at himself because he hadn't.

Several times, during the hour he stood in front of the store, he saw a shadowy movement at one of the high library windows down the block. Laurel. Checking to see what luck he was having. Or if he had left.

He felt exposed, there in full view of everyone on the street. He knew that his mother was fifty kilometres away, in one of those nifty workshops that was going to expand her options. But his dad might drive past any minute, checking out a job prospect, and see him and the duffel. He couldn't take a public quarrel, not after leaving that morning feeling so righteous and ready.

A little girl forced her mother to stop at the box.

"Could I have one?" she begged, entranced.

"They'd make great pets. Or watchdogs, or whatever," Josh said quickly, trying to cover every possibility.

The woman smiled. "How much?"

"Oh, free," Josh exclaimed. "Free. And they don't eat much at all."

The woman squeezed the little girl, almost laughing. "Which one do you like?"

The little girl picked up each puppy in turn, studying it nose to nose. The last one stretched to give her a lick. "This one," she breathed, dazzled. "He likes me already!" She turned suddenly to Josh. "We'll love it good."

"We will," the woman agreed. "Thank you."

He felt an unexpected emptiness as they walked away huddled over their treasure. He guessed it was for the puppy leaving the warmth of its brothers and sisters forever, with its little head jiggling trustfully. Or maybe it was because the woman hugged the little girl the way his father hugged him in his fantasies.

A man came out of the store. Proud of his change of luck, Josh had opened his mouth to say, "How about a beautiful puppy?" when he noticed that the tag on the man's jacket said MANAGER.

He gathered up his duffel and his dogs, and mushed.

As he passed the library, Laurel leaped out onto the top step and beckoned. "Josh! I saved some cookies for you."

He climbed up, weary. "A lady took a puppy."

Her glad smile faded. "You've only given away *one?*"

"Miss Rainey won't like me bringing them into the library, either," he said. "Have you started the party for old lady Snap Crackle Pop?"

Laurel nodded. "Grace Whipple Cox," she corrected him. "She's sitting there, waiting to autograph a stack of books taller than she is, that nobody wants to buy."

He went in, trying to be invisible behind Laurel. A tiny, round powder keg of a lady in a velvet hat sat talking to a few matronly types holding punch cups and paper napkins. He could see now why Laurel called her the Gnome de Plume, although at first she'd had to explain the pun to him. He was curious about anybody who could write poetry. He'd tried it himself. Nobody

116

knew, except Laurel, unless Miss Rainey had guessed.

Laurel led him to a little room full of magazines and gave him four pink cookies. "What'll you do now?" she asked. "Oh, Josh, they're hungry. When they're this young they need food every few hours. Could I give them some coffee-creamer stuff, do you think?"

"I don't know. Maybe not." Yips began to come from the box. He puts his jacket over it. "I've got to give them *away*. This is crazy."

"Let's try Miss Rainey," Laurel said. "I know she has cats, but maybe—" She winced as the yapping rose in a needle-sharp chorus.

He started through the door with his box and almost bull-dozed Miss Rainey off her feet as she started in.

"What on earth!" She flipped through her memory card index for his name. "Josh. What have you got?" She looked in. Her face softened. "Well bless their little defeaning hearts."

"Somebody left them under the bridge," Laurel said.

Miss Rainey breathed an angry sigh.

"I found a home for one already." Josh tilted the box so Miss Rainey would see yearning eyes and smell warm puppy. "Laurel thought maybe you'd like one."

"Oh, listen, Josh, they're already trying to zone my house as a zoo. I just couldn't. I'm gone all day. Cats and chameleons and macaws can manage. But a puppy—nope." She turned away. Then she gestured him close again, and muttered, "Try the literary ladies. It's a long shot, but try."

She was leading them out through rows of shelves, when she stopped abruptly. Every face they saw was staring at a long table of refreshments. Another of Miss Rainey's assistants, a little older than Laurel, sat at a punch bowl with her mouth ajar. Her startled eyes were riveted on a scruffy man with no socks who was helping himself to punch and cookies. His hand, the size of a baseball mitt, was already stacked with sand tarts and brownies and macaroons and six of those pink cartwheels Josh had wolfed down in the little room. The man drained his paper cup, smiled at the hypnotized girl, and refilled it. He studied his hand, and added another brownie.

Miss Rainey came alive. "Good lord—he's cleaning us out! Where did he come from?" She headed toward the man so vigorously that Josh thought she was going to grab his cookies. But she drew herself tall and said, "Sir, have you met our distinguished guest, or read her previous books of poetry?"

The scraggy man froze in his tracks. "I can't say I have," he admitted, still chewing. "But I did literally cut my teeth on poetry, ma'am. The complete unexpurgated works of Rudyard Kipling, if I remember rightly." He gave her a big shameless smile, then studied the puppies in Josh's box. "Part shepherd, wouldn't you say—the ears and head shape?"

He left Miss Rainey speechless and walked into the reference section to finish his meal in peace. The girl at the punch bowl exclaimed in a whisper, "I didn't know what to *do*, Miss Rainey! When he started loading up—"

Miss Rainey patted her shoulder mechanically. "It's all right." Her face had softened as it had when she saw the puppies. "He's hungry."

Laurel elbowed Josh toward the autographing table. A boy from high school was interviewing the Gnome de Plume, scribbling frantically at half the speed of her rushing words. Josh stopped at a distance, not wanting to interrupt but eager to get the women's attention when he could. Somebody had to take another puppy.

"Could you explain why you entitled your newest book *The Second Highest Point in Beymer County?*" the boy asked.

"To make a statement," the Gnome de Plume snapped, from behind the stack of unsold books. "Everybody knows that Crown Hill is the highest point—it's on the maps, it's written about. We act as if second-best is second-rate. I wanted to say that there can be only one topmost *anything*—all the rest of this glorious fascinating world is second. Or third, or tenth. Empty words. Hogwash. Everything has worth, for its own reasons." She knocked the mountain of books askew. "I'm not even a tenth-rate poet, although you don't have to quote me on that. I'm just a funny old lady. But why shouldn't I write a *tonne* of poetry if I want to? God doesn't label blades of grass Grade A and Grade B. He creates. For the fun of it! Because he's a creator!"

The boy had lost her, back at Crown Hill. Josh watched him write down GRADE A and take a bite of his pencil.

Two of the literary ladies, equally startled, peeped into Josh's box. Miss Rainey said, "Listen, we need homes for these abandoned little things. Someone dropped them in the river without having the decency, or the heart, to finish the job."

The ladies shook their heads sadly. One said, "A ten-to-fifteen-year commitment is too much for me. Besides, they need children to play with. A farm or something." They turned away from the box, unobtrusively putting distance also between themselves and the old lady glaring around her mountain of books.

"What's the second highest point in Beymer County?" Josh whispered.

A pink flush crossed Laurel's face. "Throne of Kings," she whispered back.

He felt his own cheeks go warm. There would never be a spot on earth higher than the Throne of Kings on an autumn day, enchanted by hawks. *Why do you have to leave me?* He wanted to beg her through the ache in his throat.

But he was leaving first. You do it to them before they do it to you. You don't just stand there on the reject pile, smiling like it doesn't hurt.

The grungy guy tapped him on the shoulder. "You say you're giving pups away?" His cookies were gone, except for the frosting on his beard.

Josh nodded, surprised.

"I'll take one," the man said.

Everyone looked at Josh. The man put his paper cup on the stack of books. It looked like a lighthouse.

"Oh," Miss Rainey said. "I don't think—" She stopped, flustered.

"I don't know," Josh said carefully. "I mean—I don't know

you." He hadn't known the woman with the little girl, either, he remembered. "Aren't you just—on the road? I mean, if you don't have a job or anything, how could you feed it, and all?"

"I live here," the man said. "Hey, I wouldn't take it if I couldn't come up with the goods. I take care of *me*, don't I? What's your name? I look like I can manage to take care of a pup, don't I?"

"Josh," he told him, nodding in spite of his doubts.

"Joshua fit the battle of Jericho," the man said, as if he had the habit of telling himself things. "Well, Josh, you trust me or you don't. It's a risk."

"I don't know," Josh said in desperation. How could he tell? What kind of life would a puppy have with a man like that?

But what did it take to beat dying in a box by the river?

Suddenly the man grubbed in the pocket of his ragged pea jacket and brought out a pencil in a handful of lint and crumbs. "I'll tell you what, Josh, my friend, I'll give you my address. You come check on me. Check on your pup—see if I don't do a commendable job on it." He handed Josh a napkin with a street number on it. There were no houses there, Josh knew from his paper route days. A warehouse. So? Guard dogs stayed in warehouses okay. The man gave him a half glance with wary watery eyes. He's begging, Josh thought. It's rough by yourself.

He held out the box. "Which one do you want?"

The man said softly, "The runt." He lifted out the smallest puppy, smoothing its fuzzy head with his thumb. He said, "You keep that address. You come out and check."

"I will," Josh warned him. "You better be telling me the truth."

The man tucked the puppy inside his jacket. "I'll be gentle with it, Josh, my friend. I had a belt taken to me too many times to ever lift my hand to another creature."

He bowed to the ladies, smiling, and went out.

The Gnome de Plume thrust a book into Laurel's hand. "Run catch him," she ordered. Her squinty old eyes glinted with what looked to Josh like pleasure.

Laurel darted out. Josh felt a spurt of happiness. Two pups down—three to go. The rest of March, April, May before Laurel left. They'd go to the Throne of Kings again, and this time he would be able to say, *I'm glad we knew each other and liked and loved each other. Even if it can't be the way I wanted it to be.*

The Gnome de Plume brought a box from under the table and began to fill it with her books. The ladies gathered to help.

Josh was folding the napkin into his pocket when his hand froze. What was he doing? He wasn't going to be here to check on anybody's address. He was going to be out there on a bus. Finding his own warehouse to sleep in. There wouldn't be another day on the Throne of Kings. Never another day. He slung his head, blinking as if he'd run into a door in the dark.

He went out blindly and stood on the sidewalk, breathing hard. The box of puppies, lighter now, bulged and bumped in his hands. Laurel came back and stood beside him. They watched the cars go by in the long afternoon shadows.

"Were you just saying that?" she asked, with a pinched, anxious smile. "When you told him you'd check on the puppy?"

A car like dad's came toward them. He went tight. It passed, driven by a boy in a baseball cap. Josh let out his breath. His voice, sounding far away, said, "Just once, if my folks would just look up and notice I was there. That's all it would take."

Laurel nodded. She always nodded, understanding, and he always went on explaining and defending himself, like some kind of neglected machine grinding itself to pieces.

"I mean, they talk to me—sure—but they're doing other things while they're yelling at me. Like I was some emergency they wished they weren't having."

Grace Whipple Cox came out the door with a load of books. Miss Rainey followed with another box and the last of the cookies under plastic on a wobbly paper plate.

"Let me carry that," Laurel said, taking the Gnome's load. Josh set the puppies down and took the books and plate from Miss Rainey. They followed the Gnome down the chilly street to her beat-up car and put the boxes in the back.

"Not much of an afternoon, dollar-wise," she said. He didn't understand why she followed them back to the library. She looked down at the puppies. "I wish I was sure I *had* ten-to-fifteen years to commit," she said, and laughed. "But so what? We can't wait for life to be perfect, can we?" She lifted up two puppies.

He heard Laurel draw a soft breath.

The Gnome de Plume said, "I can't take all three—I'm tempting fate as it is. But fate has sent them a guardian angel once already." She smiled at Josh. "Fate can do it again, if I don't last long enough. And they'll have each other." She bent closer. "Would you like one of my books?"

He gulped. "Yes," he told her, taking it. "I would."

The Gnome smiled at Laurel and handed her the puppies. "Come, young lady. I'll drive you home."

Laurel turned to Josh. Her anxious eyes tried to read his. "Your duffel is in the little room."

"I know," he said. He didn't move.

Slowly she started after the Gnome. "Josh?" she entreated, looking back.

"It won't work," he said. "I go home—they're madder than ever—we start yelling—"

"Part of that's up to you, isn't it?" she asked.

Her soft words let him down with a thump. Dang—*help* me, he wanted to yell. Don't just pile it back on me.

"Josh, can't you try? We have to get through things the best we can." Her voice was shaking. "I'll listen and listen, if it'll help, but it's up to you finally."

He turned away. Inside the library he stared through the window as the Gnome's car, and then others, and then others, passed in the dusk.

His dad was watching the news. He asked, "Where've you been?" without turning from the TV.

Josh felt the eeriness start again, matching the jumpy light of the screen that lit the room. He took the puppy out of his jacket. It seemed like fate, really, because the one that had been left was the one whose tender eyes had grabbed his heart beside the river.

"What's that?" his dad said, when he noticed. "You can't keep a dog. Your mother's got too much to do already."

"She won't have to take care of it," Josh said, keeping his voice even and slow. "I will. Feeding and housebreaking and shots and tags and spaying and everything."

His dad looked at him a long time. "Talk is cheap," he said.

"I guess you're going to have to risk it," Josh said, braced against the gaze.

His dad turned back to the news. "She can't do everything. The house, her schooling. She's got big dreams for herself. Give her a chance."

The puppy tried to crawl inside Josh's collar. He had to feed it. He had to buy a bag of something. "I live here too," he said. He felt for his ticket money. Maybe if he called Laurel she'd walk to the store with him and carry the pup while he lugged home a bag of dog chow. And they could talk. "Give me a chance too. Okay?"

His dad switched channels uneasily, testing, rejecting. He doesn't know how to answer me, Josh thought. He doesn't know what to say to any of this—to not having a job, or to her getting ahead of him, or to being my father.

A commercial came on. His dad said, watching it, "When I went into the army my folks kept my dog for me. They said he got lost. Ran away. But I was never sure." His face slowly warped in the shifting light. "Maybe he tried to find me. Or maybe he got killed and they hated to tell me. So I never could be sure, you know? For a long time I used to listen to the dogs barking, off in town. For years, I guess. Hoping I'd hear him."

Josh stopped halfway to the door. Hesitantly he came back, and sat on the arm of the couch, stroking the hungry puppy with his thumb. He stared at the television like his dad, not seeing it. Even with the sound turned high, he caught himself trying to hear other things. The far-off whine of buses. The almost unaudible cries and urgings and answers coming from everywhere.

What is justice? Who should decide what's fair? What happens when people take justice into their own hands? If you think you know the answers, this unit may make you think again.

DOUBTS ABOUT SELF-DEFENCE

Malcolm Gray

In New York City four young men are shot and wounded in a subway by the man they are trying to rob. Two years later a Calgary pharmacist discovers a man trying to steal money and drugs and kills him with a shotgun blast as the robber flees. The incidents are unrelated—or are they? This June 1987 article raises many questions about North Americans' views of justice, self-defence, guilt, and innocence.

A man who sparked a widespread debate over the use and limits of deadly force in self-defence remained secluded in a New York City highrise apartment building last week—all but imprisoned by continuing interest in his case. Outside the West 14th Street building, crowds of reporters waited in hope of obtaining an interview with Bernhard Goetz. He is the bespectacled 39-year-old electrical engineer who shot and wounded four young black men on a crowded subway car in December, 1984—in the belief, he said, that they were about to attack and rob him. Last week a jury of ten whites and two blacks acquitted him of attempted murder charges arising from that incident—a verdict that some U.S. black community leaders said endorsed vigilantism. And in Calgary, strikingly similar issues arose at the trial of drugstore owner Steven Kesler, facing second-degree murder charges after a man was gunned down outside his pharmacy during a robbery attempt last November.

In that incident, Kesler, 41, allegedly chased 27-year-old Timothy Smith into 21st Street S.E. and killed him with a blast from a shotgun. But when police charged Kesler, public response in Calgary paralleled the expression of support that Goetz received from many U.S. citizens after the subway shooting. But although fellow store owners and hundreds of other Calgary residents raised more than $37 000 to pay his legal expenses, city police spokesmen expressed their concern at the reaction to the slaying. Declared Supt. Frank Mitchell last November: "The police are here so the individual citizen doesn't have to get involved in gunfights." Similarly, New York officials warned that anyone taking the law into his own hands would face prosecution. Still, Roger Green, a Democratic state assembly member from Brooklyn who is also chairman of the 25-member Black and Puerto Rican Legislative Caucus in Albany, N.Y., stated that the jury's decision "sanctions dangerous vigilante actions on the part of misguided citizens."

Several jurors in the Goetz trial defended their finding in subsequent interviews—and stressed that the verdict did not condone rough justice in a city plagued by racial friction and street crime. According to one juror, 28-year-old computer programmer Mark Lesly, all twelve jury members concluded that Goetz had not committed a serious offence. Lesly also said that the jury believed that the defendant—who had been the victim of an earlier robbery on the subway—thought that he faced a deadly threat when four youths with sharpened screwdrivers in their possession approached him and asked for five dollars. Said Lesly: "People may think that this gives licence to go out and shoot black people, but the fact is that those four people were a deadly threat to Goetz—black, white or whatever."

In the same way, defence lawyer James Ogle told an Alberta Court of Queen's Bench jury last week that a series of robberies and break-ins at his client's store had driven Kesler to arm himself. In the thirty months before the shooting incident, said Ogle, burglars had twice broken into the store and stolen drugs—and armed robbers seeking narcotics had held up Kesler on two occasions during that same period. In one incident, according to Kesler, a masked man who demanded all the narcotics in the store pointed a handgun at his wife, Mary, and threatened to kill her. And in a robbery that occurred six months before the fatal shooting, a robber struck Kesler on the head with a gun.

Speaking from the stand in his own defence, the dark-haired drugstore owner said that he had kicked one of the robbers in the face in an unsuccessful attempt to stop the man from leaving with the drugs. According to Kesler, those hold-ups convinced him and his wife that their lives were in danger. Said Kesler: "We realized that our lives had become very unsafe, that it was a very fine line between staying alive or being killed by robbers." Still, he flatly denied earlier trial testimony by Calgary Det. Paul Manuel. According to Manuel, Kesler had told him that he had purchased a shotgun after the hold-ups and break-ins—and promised that he would shoot to kill the next person who attempted to rob his store.

Indeed, Kesler's lawyer said that the shooting had occurred "in a blind panic under a stressful situation, a situation of great fear." That description is similar to the arguments that Goetz's lawyers presented. And, like Kesler, their client is still entangled in the consequences of a shooting incident. He still must face sentencing in September on the single conviction returned by the jury: illegally possessing the .38-calibre revolver used in the incident. Goetz will learn then if he is to spend time in prison, or avoid jail entirely. In a Calgary courtroom, a slightly built drugstore owner waits for a judge and jury to make a similar ruling on his destiny.

NIGHT OF THE TWISTER

James Michael Ullman

All afternoon the air had been humid and oddly still, with the temperature hovering in the thirties. Old-timers, wiping their brows and gazing at dark thunderheads gathering in the southwestern sky, knew they were in for trouble.

At dusk, as thunder cracked and rain pelted down in blinding sheets, the trouble came in the form of whirling, funnel-shaped clouds.

One tornado ripped through a mobile-home court, killing five people. Another flattened every structure in a whistle-stop on the Saint Louis-San Francisco Railway, and a third blew a sedan off a county road, fatally injuring its occupant.

At least a dozen funnel clouds had been sighted by 9:08 p.m., at which time a tall, dark-haired woman walked from the kitchen of a remote farmhouse into the parlour. She thought she'd heard a car in the front yard. Her imagination probably. Nobody in his right mind would be out driving on a wild night like this.

She started toward a window but never made it.

Someone kicked the front door open, springing the lock, and two men stumbled in. Both carried pistols.

The taller and older of the two swung the bore of his weapon toward the young woman's midsection and said, "Freeze, lady. Anyone else in this house?"

Wordlessly she shook her head.

"Okay. You can sit down now. But be nice and quiet, and keep your hands at your sides."

Slowly she eased into a chair.

The room's only light came from kerosene lamps. The power had gone out long ago. From the kitchen, music wafted faintly from a transistor radio.

The two intruders, bareheaded, with crew cuts, were dressed in soaking wet blue-denim uniforms.

"Jerry, close that door," the older man ordered. "Then see if there's anyone else here. She might be lying."

Jerry, a thin, short youth of about twenty, hesitated a moment to stare at the young woman. Then he slammed the front door, braced it with a table, and took off to search the house.

The other man walked around behind the woman. He had broad shoulders, a flat belly, a hawklike profile, and dark rings under eyes that burned with an abnormal intensity. His age could have been anywhere between thirty-five and fifty.

Placing the pistol's muzzle to the woman's head, he asked, "What's your name?"

"Karen." Terrified, she worked hard at keeping her voice steady. Her intuition told her that any display of panic might trigger violence against her person. "Karen Smallwood."

"Who lives here with you?"

"I don't live here. My parents do, but they're away. I'm a teacher—I live in town. I came out to straighten up for them but got caught by the storm."

"We're lost. We were on County B, headed for Hanksville and the Interstate when we hit a washout. We had to detour onto the cowpath that took us here. Where's it go?"

"Same place as County B—to Hanksville—only it takes a few minutes longer to get there."

"Any bridges in between?"

"No, there'll be no more washouts."

"Driving to this farm, we were going up a hill. What's on the other side? Another farm?"

"Not right away. Nobody lives within five kilometres of here."

"If you been listening to that radio, you must know who we are. Except for the tornadoes, we been the big story."

"Yes," she said. "I know. I don't remember your name."

"Garth," he said pleasantly. "Ben Garth."

"You and your friend broke out of prison yesterday. The police in half the country are looking for you."

She didn't bother adding what they both knew very well: that Garth had been serving a sentence for murder, Jerry for rape; that since breaking out, they had shot and killed a motorist, whose car they had stolen, and then beaten a waitress to death in a roadside diner. The newscaster had termed it a "senseless killing spree."

Jerry came back. "There's nobody else," he reported, "but I found this."

He held a faded photograph of Karen, then a leggy teenager, and a middle-aged couple. The man in the picture wore a state police uniform.

"The cop your father?" Garth asked.

"Yes," she admitted. "But he isn't a trooper anymore. He was hurt chasing a speeder, so they pensioned him off."

"Where are your folks now?"

"A flea market in Canton, Texas. They won't be back until next week."

"A what?"

"Flea market," she repeated. "A place where anyone can go and sell anything. My folks barely make out on my father's pension. As a sideline, they sell antiques. Just look around..."

Garth scrutinized the home's interior more closely. She was right. The parlour and dining room looked more like an antique store than a farmhouse. Pictures in Victorian frames hung from walls; shelves and cupboards were filled with china and glassware; the floor areas were jammed with heavy old chairs and tables.

"You're pretty cool about all this," Garth said. "I admire

women who don't lose their heads and start hollerin', like the one in the diner this mornin'—the one we had to shut up."

He didn't admire her. He was probing, wondering how much she could take.

"There's no point in screaming," Karen said as casually as she could, "if nobody but you two would hear."

"Smart girl. Just in case the storm gets worse, you got a storm cellar in this place?"

"The door's in the kitchen floor."

Jerry went to the kitchen, lifted the door, and swung a kerosene lantern down for a better look. "It's no fancy hotel," he called back, "but we could sweat it out if we had to."

"Any guns in this house?" Garth went on. "If your old man was a cop, he must have some guns."

"Two hunting rifles, a shotgun, and two revolvers," she replied without hesitation. "They're locked in a case upstairs. My father has the key, but if you want them you can just break the glass."

"We'll take 'em when we leave."

"You were wise," Karen said, "ditching your car to find shelter. A car's the worst place to be if a twister hits."

She said that to get Garth's mind off guns. She didn't want him thinking about guns because there was one she hadn't mentioned, an ancient double-barreled shotgun hanging in plain sight on the wall over the mantel in the dining room.

Apparently it was now nothing more than a decorative but useless antique; it hung so high that to get it, she'd have to climb up on a chair to lift it off its brackets.

While it was antique, it was not useless, however. Despite its age it was loaded and in perfect working condition. That old shotgun, her father had said, would be his ace in the hole. He hoped he'd never need it, but as a former law officer living far out in the country, and knowing some men held grudges against him, he wanted an emergency weapon.

At the moment, though, it seemed the shotgun would not do Karen much good. It was difficult to imagine the circumstances under which Garth would allow her to climb the chair, reach up, and turn the weapon on her captors....

Garth took the pistol away from Karen's head and jammed it under his belt. "Okay," he drawled. "we ain't ate since mornin', and I never been fed by a lawman's daughter before. So you just haul into that kitchen and fix us somethin'—fast."

The men drank beer and watched her every move as she prepared a quick supper of frankfurters and canned beans. As they ate, they made her sit across the dining-room table from them—the shotgun on the wall behind them.

When they were through, Karen cleared the table and brought more beer. On the radio, the announcer reported the sighting of more funnel clouds.

"I don't suppose," Karen said, settling back in her chair, "either of you has ever seen a tornado."

"No, I ain't," Garth said. "And I don't hanker to."

Jerry asked, "Have you?"

"Yes."

"What's it like?"

She thought back to that terrifying afternoon so many years ago. "It's a black, whirling piece of hell, that's what. They say the funnel's wind moves so fast it can drive a splinter of wood into your brain like a high-powered bullet. And pieces of glass—God help you if you're near a window. You'll be cut to ribbons."

Uneasily, Jerry glanced at the broad expanse of windows in the dining room. "Then it's dangerous just sitting here. We should be down in the cellar, like the radio said."

"It's a little dangerous," Karen conceded. "If a twister dipped down from the sky to exactly this spot, we'd be finished. But if it's already on the ground and moving toward you, you'll probably know it and have warning. Even if it's night and you can't see the twister, you can hear it."

"I read about that," Jerry told her. "They make a noise."

"Yes. Like a freight train. The time I heard that sound I was in open country. I looked up and there it was, bearing down on me. There was a ditch nearby, and I had enough sense to climb into a culvert. Even so, it's a miracle I lived through it. You know what happens sometimes? The funnels pick people up and pull them so high into the sky that when they drop down, they're frozen solid. And then at other times they simply—"

"That's enough." Garth frowned. Apparently the talk about tornadoes was making him edgy. "I don't wanna hear no more about it."

Again he looked around the house. This time his perusal was slower and more thorough. His gaze even paused briefly at the ancient shotgun before moving on. He asked, "Any money around here?"

"Only a few dollars in my purse. My father never leaves cash in the house when he's going out of town."

"Uh-huh." Garth turned to Jerry. "Get it. Then go through the rest of this place. See if there's more stashed away."

Rummaging through Karen's purse, Jerry came up with a few bills and coins. "Four dollars and thirty-five cents," he said in disgust. "That won't take us far...."

He shoved the money into his pocket and began ransacking the house, sweeping shelves clean, pulling out drawers, and dumping their contents onto the floor. It was part search and part pure vandalism, random destruction for its own sake. Karen compressed her lips to keep from crying out as the boy smashed the collections of porcelain, glassware, and other fragile artifacts her parents had spent so much of their time assembling. When Jerry was through on the ground floor, he went upstairs. They could hear him tramping around, smashing more things.

Watching Karen while sipping from still another can of beer, Garth smiled humourlessly. Even the modest amount of alcohol in the beer seemed to be having a bad effect on his mood. Clearly she was dealing with a highly unstable psychopath, likely to go berserk upon little or no provocation.

Jerry returned with only a few more coins for his efforts.

"I told you," Karen said patiently, "my father doesn't keep money here."

"Yeah." Garth was looking at her in an odd way. "Too bad. If he had, we'd be more friendly inclined. We need money to get out of the country."

"I'm sorry."

"Teacher, you just *think* you're sorry. But before we're through with you, you'll *really* be sorry."

He was tormenting her verbally before getting around to the real thing. She had to stall him as long as possible. "Why would you want to hurt me?" She tried to sound friendly and reasonable. "I haven't made any trouble. I've done everything you asked."

"Maybe just because you're a lawman's daughter. We got an abiding dislike for lawmen and anyone connected with 'em. Matter of fact, we don't much like teachers either. Do we, Jerry?"

The boy grinned at her vacuously. She'd get no help from that quarter.

"It wouldn't make sense anyhow," Garth went on, "leavin' you here alive. The police think we're a few hundred kilometres north of here. But the first thing you'd do after we left would be to put 'em straight."

"You could lock me in the storm cellar. That'd give you plenty of time for a head start."

"Nope. Can't take chances. We'll lock you in the storm cellar, all right, but when we do you won't be in no condition to climb out. Not ever. That way, we *know* we'll have a head start. It might be a long time before anyone gets curious enough to bust in to see why you ain't been around lately."

Despite the fear tearing at her insides, Karen managed a smile. "You're just trying to frighten me. You're playing games. Well, sure I'm scared. What girl wouldn't be? But you know you don't have to kill me, Garth. If you don't want to leave me, take me along. I won't try anything stupid. I'll...." She paused. "Just a minute. You hear that?"

Garth stood up. "Hear what?"

"Shut up," Jerry broke in, his grin gone. "I hear it, too."

Then there was no doubt. They all heard it, far off but coming closer, a growing clatter and roar suggestive of an approaching freight train.

Karen rose. "I don't know about you," she announced, "but while there's still time, I'm going into that storm cellar!"

She took a step forward, but Jerry lunged ahead, shoving her aside. Garth hesitated a moment and then, as the sound mounted in intensity, he plunged after Jerry.

As they scrambled for the door in the kitchen floor, Karen climbed up on the chair. She lifted the shotgun from its rack, stepped down, cocked the piece, aimed it while shoving the stock tight against her shoulder, and braced herself against the wall.

As Garth looked up and clawed for his pistol, she squeezed one trigger and then the other....

At dawn, her face expressionless, Karen watched from a parlour window as Garth's body was loaded into a hearse. The blasts had killed him almost instantly. Jerry had been seriously wounded but would live.

Standing beside Karen, a state police detective said, "I know how you feel. No matter how justified, it's terrible to kill someone. But you had no choice. If you hadn't stopped them, they'd almost surely have killed you and others."

"I know. Thinking about that is the only way I'll be able to live with this."

"Anyhow either you were mighty lucky or they were mighty careless, allowing you to get your hands on the gun."

"Oh, that." She smiled faintly. "At the time they were trying to get into the storm cellar. I'd told them how a tornado sounded like a fast freight train." Her gaze strayed beyond the yard to the other side of the hill and the main line of the Saint Louis-San Francisco Railway. "So when the night freight came highballing by a little before ten, like it always does, I made out like it was a twister."

THE HUNTSMAN

David Lewis Stein

The boy, Luscoe, lay on his back in the sun, with seven golf balls spread out on the grass before him. A skinny, sunbrowned boy with bright eyes and an eager innocent face, he wore only blue jeans belted tightly over his hipless waist, and a faded yellow T-shirt.

Below him on the green, the golfers had almost finished their putts. He scanned them, one hand over his eyes, trying to decide from their walk and the cut of their clothes whether they would buy from him. The seven shiny white globes, cleaned and polished, were the fruits of his morning's work. He had found them in two short hours of combing the brush at the side of the sixteenth hole. If he sold them now, the profit would enable him to eat lunch early.

The first golfer approached, a fat sombre man who bore his golf club like a swagger-stick tucked up under his arm. He examined each ball carefully, running his fingers over it for cracks. He completely ignored the boy stretched out in front of him. The merchandise was divided into two groups with one good ball in each group. Luscoe watched the man's face. It remained expressionless. At last the golfer spoke, still holding the ball in his hand but without looking at the boy.

"How much?" he said. His voice was smooth and hard, like a school principal's.

"A dollar for three and a dollar for four." Luscoe rose and backed a metre or so away from the man.

"Not worth it."

"They're good balls."

"Only one good ball in the lot. Give you a quarter for it."

"I got to sell them in groups, mister."

"Crocks're no good to me." He tucked the golf club back under his arm and strode off to the tee to join his friends. Luscoe lay down again and placed his head in his cupped hands. The sun was bright and warm on his face. He thought about the golfer. Sometimes they were like that and other times they were good and bought everything he had. That was one of the risks he took. There were other risks too, like the days he looked for hours among the bushes and rocks and found nothing, and the old ranger employed by the course specifically to guard against boys like Luscoe. But Luscoe endured these risks with silent patience, because above all things he loved to hunt for golf balls. It was not the money, for his needs were small; and it was not the freedom, for he had never in his life felt the least restraint. It was rather something deep and quiet that he could taste like meat in his mouth, when his feet moved in a circular swishing motion through the grass and suddenly, without seeing or feeling anything in particular, he bent down and pulled a golf ball out from under a dead leaf or a tuft of grass. He seemed always to know the placed to look and when to stop and where to run his hand over the dried mud where a sunken golf ball was just a white dot in the rigid earth. He knew every clump of trees and stretch of land on the course and just how to cover it properly.

There were now two women golfers on the green, portly ladies who played the game with grim intensity. He watched them closely and decided they would buy. When the first came he rose and stood demurely behind his wares, like a clerk in a dry-goods store. She stopped and smiled at him. The second woman came up to them, pulling a golf cart behind her. She took a score card from the pocket of her skirt and began to figure on it with a pencil, oblivious to her companion and to Luscoe. The first picked up a ball and began to examine it.

"How much do you want for these, son?" she asked.

"A dollar for each group, ma'am." Luscoe's tone was quiet and respectful.

"What do you think, Aggie?"

Aggie looked up from her score-card. "Don't know," she said. "It's your money."

"I'll take them," said the first woman. "I'll take them all. Both groups."

She reached into her purse for a wallet and gave two bills to the child. Aggie watched, tapping her fingers impatiently on her scorecard. The buyer gathered her seven balls and both women went off to the tee. Luscoe watched them drive off.

The sun was now overhead and he decided to eat lunch. He began to cut diagonally across the fairways, moving with a loose, graceful trot. When he saw a golfer about to hit he would freeze motionless, his hands clenched tightly at his sides, until he heard the dull thump of the ball and saw the direction of the bounce. Then he would move on.

At the juncture of three holes there was a refreshment booth, tended by a waiter from the club house. No matter what the weather the waiter, whose name was Carl, wore a starched white jacket and a black bow tie. There were some golfers finishing bottles of soda in front of the booth, so Luscoe waited until they were finished and then approached.

"How's tricks?" said the waiter.

Luscoe always bought his lunchtime drink at the booth and over the months he and Carl had become good friends. They had an arrangement whereby he purchased most of Luscoe's stock and disposed of it somewhere in the mysteries of the club house. Sometimes the waiter would save pieces of pastry from the club house and bring them to the boy.

"Have you got a ginger ale?"

"Coming up!" He took a bottle from the cooler and opened it with a flourish.

"And a pack of cigarettes." Luscoe was feeling good. The waiter gave him some filter tips.

"Have you got anything for me today?" His face was wide and smiling. Luscoe suddenly felt bad. He knew he should have saved something for Carl, even though the waiter never paid the prices he got from golfers on the course. Still they were friends.

"Everything I find this afternoon," said Luscoe after a pause, "I'll bring to you."

"That's my boy," Carl said. "People up at the club house ask me and I tell them I got a friend down on the course can find them all they can use." He reached over and pinched Luscoe's cheeks.

The child turned his eyes to the ground and smiled. Then he gathered up his ginger ale and shoved the cigarettes into his back pocket.

"I'll be back at six o'clock," he said. "Before you close up."

"See you later. And maybe I'll have something special for you if the truck comes out again." He gave the departing boy a huge wink.

Luscoe's favourite spot for eating was the top of a hill from which he could look down on almost the whole course: the long line of unblemished fairways to his left, and to his right, a line of trees descending into bushes and leading to a creek and then the ranger's car with the ranger sunning himself on the running board. The ranger seldom did anything else. From time to time he would make a little tour of the holes nearest him, pausing to scan the distant rough with an old pair of binoculars, and sometimes he talked to the players, but he was an old man and mostly he preferred to sit in the sun.

Luscoe took two sandwiches from his pocket and ate methodically, spacing the sips from his ginger ale so that he had almost half the bottle to wash his mouth out when he had finished. Then he heaved the bottle against a rock and lit one of the cigarettes. He didn't inhale, but smoked because he liked the bitter taste in his mouth.

From his high perch he seemed to look down on another, more perfect world. The greens were a different type of grass than the fairways and they glowed with a rich lustre in the afternoon heat. The trees, in sombre single file between the holes, divided the course with austere dignity into logical rows. The golfers, distant, barely animate dots in the overwhelming green, scarcely disturbed the bright tranquility of the scene. There was over all a tangible quality of peace that he loved.

He finished his cigarette and decided to work the creek for the afternoon. The creek was really an irrigation ditch that ran diagonally across the course. At one point it lay on the bottom of the deep valley, with the tee on one side and the green on the other. Luscoe found this particular spot ideal for hunting.

He took off his shoes and socks and put them in a clump of grass on the bank. The water was bitterly cold. It came well above his knees and lapped at the rolled cuffs of his jeans. He stood shivering for several seconds until the shock abated and then began to thread his way along one bank. His feet moved in slow sensitive arcs, describing circles as he advanced. It was not easy to hunt in the creek. The solid lumps that remained still long enough for you to wrap your toes around them usually turned out to be stones. It was the delicate brushings, that barely touched your feet, that were the golf balls. Luscoe, as he wound tightly through the water, seemed almost to be listening for something. He followed the contours of one side until the creek disappeared into an irrigation pipe, and then turned and began to work his way back along the opposite side.

As he neared the place where his shoes were hidden a shadow fell across him and the water. He paused, staring at the darkness on the water ahead of him, and then looked up. Two older boys were standing on the bank directly above him. They seemed to have been there a long time, watching him. One was holding a golf club in his right hand, and swinging it aimlessly at the dandelions around him.

"How you doing?" he said to Luscoe. His manner seemed open and relaxed.

"Not bad. I found five balls here in the creek." The child watched their faces.

"You want to sell?" said the other. His face was red and pimply.

"I promised these to the man who runs the booth."

"Sell them to us. We'll see that he gets them."

"Can't. I promised to bring them myself."

The boy with the golf club squatted down until he was looking directly into Luscoe's eyes. "Look, kid," he said, "I might as well be honest with you. We're taking over, see? We're gonna organize things around here for you and for everybody. But you gotta sell to us. See that car?"—he jerked his thumb over his shoulder—"That's ours, and we can cover a lot of territory with it."

Luscoe looked behind the boy. There was an old model T parked on the hill above the hole. The other boy bent down beside his friend until the two of them were facing the child.

"This is gonna be all right for everybody," he said. "We buy from you and we sell around the different courses. With our car we can go anywhere. Everybody makes money."

"How much will you give me for these?" Luscoe took the five golf balls from his pocket.

The boy with the golf club examined them without picking them up. "Fifty cents," he said.

"But they're worth more!"

"You gotta remember kid, we got a lotta expenses to cover."

Luscoe put the balls back in his pocket. "I don't think I want to sell to you," he said, pronouncing his words slowly like a school teacher.

Both boys stood up. The pimply-faced one picked up Luscoe's shoes and held them at arm's length over the creek.

"You sell to us, kid, or we drop your shoes!" His voice was suddenly hard and vicious. Luscoe felt himself swimming through some incomprehensible dream. If he could only shake his head at the right moment all this would vanish and things would be good again.

"How about it, kid?" He was holding the shoes between his thumb and forefinger. He seemed casual and unconcerned, as if it was no matter to him which way Luscoe decided.

"It's up to you kid."

"But I can make more money selling to Carl or to the golfers!"

Luscoe looked wildly about him but there was no one else in sight. There was no sound but the sinister swishing of the golf club as it clipped the dandelion heads. The two boys watched him dispassionately. He took the balls out of his side pocket and laid them on the bank. The pimply-faced boy gathered them up and gave him two quarters. Luscoe clasped his hands around them without a word.

"Remember," said the other boy, "if you want to work around here again, you sell to us." He dropped the shoes into the creek. The socks floated up to the top. Before Luscoe could think or act, the two boys turned and walked up to their old car. Luscoe began to cry, hot angry tears that he did not try to stop. He felt with his feet until he found his shoes and gathered his socks from the brown crest of the water. He sat on the bank and put them on. The tears were like a pane of frosted glass before his eyes, so thick that he could barely see to tie the laces.

He trudged across the course, heedless of the players and the occasional flying golf ball. His feet left soggy imprints as he went. He never once looked back. At the dinner table he only played with his food and when his mother tried to find out what was wrong he scowled at her. She sent him off to bed. Later, in the sanctuary of his room, he lay on his back staring up at the ceiling. There was no light but from time to time the headlights of a passing car would throw a pattern on the wall. He played over and over again in his mind the events of the day. He knew he must do something, but he also knew that it had been for him, thus far, too perfect. Outside the door he heard his family mounting the stairs to go to bed and later, the clicking of lights and then the house was quiet. He lay motionless and then it came to him, so sudden and so simple that it seemed he had known it all along. He slept.

It rained the next morning but by noon it had cleared up and the sun began to come out. Luscoe remained at home, in his room, working on a model airplane. He left the door closed and his mother and family did not disturb him. At about two o'clock he put on his rubber boots and windbreaker and went off to the course. He did not tell anyone where he was going.

The ground was wet and a light mist hung over the fairways. There were few golfers. Luscoe tramped through the trees with his hands in his pockets. He did not look at the ground and his feet made no swishing motions through the grass. By the seventh hole, parked under a tree, he found the ranger's car. He crouched behind a bush for several minutes until he was certain the old man was inside, and then heaved a stone that bounced off the car's windshield. The old man stumbled out and began to peer intently into the bush. Luscoe ran away.

He ran all the way to the hole where he had encountered the two boys the day before. They were down in the valley working the creek, his creek. He laughed and began to hum to himself. Their car was parked behind the green on a slight incline. Still humming to himself, Luscoe opened the door and released the emergency brake. The car began to move slightly. He went around to the back and began to push. The speed increased. At the top of the hill the car seemed to pause, to hesitate, almost to stop, and then it fell. The two boys stood knee-deep in the creek watching it come, helpless, struck dumb by the spectacle approaching. The car gathered momentum as it descended, the tires cutting wide ruts in the soft earth. And then it struck a tree, turned over, slid sideways and came to a stop, half-submerged in the creek. The two boys remained where they were, paralyzed in the water. From the top of the hill Luscoe could see the ranger approaching. He turned away and went home.

For two days he did not return. He stayed in his room humming to himself and finishing his model airplane. Every time he thought of the car he laughed out loud. Finally on the third day he decided to hunt again, and came back to the course. It was a clean, bright sunshiny day. The air was so pure it seemed to cut his nostrils. At the seventh hole, his favourite, he began his sweeping movements through the bushes and grass. His eyes, his whole body, seemed focused on the immediate piece of ground in front of him. From time to time he paused to pocket a ball. It seemed to be a good morning. And then he felt it rather than saw it and began to run. The footsteps of the man ran with him. "Stop! Stop!" the voice kept saying. Luscoe did not look back. He was moving up a hill and as he advanced the panting steps grew dimmer. At the top they seemed to have gone back completely. Luscoe paused, breathless, and looked back. Below him a young man in a ranger's uniform was shaking his fist.

"Don't come back!" he shouted. "Don't ever come back or we'll put you in jail!" His face was puffy, red and mean. Luscoe watched him turn and stride away. His walk had an arrogant military swing to it. He leaned against a tree, utterly incapable of movement, waiting for his panting to subside. Time seemed to pass through and around the child. The man had worn a ranger's uniform but he was not the ranger. He was young and vigorous.

Luscoe set out through the trees to find his friend Carl. The booth was deserted. The waiter was seated on an upturned soda case, reading a newspaper. The child approached stealthily. Carl looked up.

"What are you doing here, boy?" he said. The waiter seemed shocked and surprised to see him. Luscoe could see nothing startling in his appearance.

"What's wrong, Carl? Why shouldn't I be here?"

"Haven't you heard?"

"Heard what? I've been sick for two days."

"About them two guys with the car. They were hunting balls up at the twelfth and left the brake off. Car rolled down the hill. Boy, what a mess! We had to get a big tow truck to get it out. Lucky one of the kids' old man was a member so they didn't go to court, but they still got to pay for everything."

"But how does that bother me?" Luscoe could not help smiling to himself when he thought of the two boys and the tow truck.

"They got three new rangers and the old man. They're going to prosecute every guy they catch. You better learn to caddy, boy!"

"But I don't want to caddy!"

"Well, you won't be doing much hunting around here. Not anymore."

Carl sat down again on his case and began to read his newspaper. Luscoe waited for him to say something more but the man remained silent. The child moved a short distance away and then turned to look back. The waiter did not look up. Luscoe took the golf balls from his pocket and heaved them into the bush. Then he went home.

Boy still meets girl, and girl still meets boy, but the rules have changed a little. In the following pages three writers take a humorous look at modern love.

HANDLING TEEN CALLS

Gary Lautens

The other evening the telephone rang and a lovely female voice asked, "Is Stephen there?"

As it happened, he wasn't, so I said, "I'm sorry, he's out."

I should have left it at that.

However, I broke the cardinal rule of being the father of a teenager while answering a telephone.

"Is that Debbie?" I asked.

Boom, crash and thud.

As soon as the words were out I knew I had made a terrible mistake.

"No," was the rather chilly reply. "It's..."

Of course it was a totally different name, the name of somebody who obviously didn't know Debbie even exists or, if she did, wasn't happy about it.

What a fool I am.

With three teenagers in the house, I should know you never mention a name over the phone and give away a son's (or daughter's) secrets.

You say, "Hello, there" or, "Hi, I'm sorry but you missed Stephen. Is there any message?" You can even say, "He's out but he won't be long."

But you don't cough up a free name and put your teenager in possible hot water with someone he's probably told is the only one in his life.

When will I learn?

I am pretty good now in that I never say, when a teenager at our house gets a call, "He (or she) is in the bathroom. I'll take a message."

Bathroom references are "gross."

Also, I never say, "He's over at Bill's. You might reach him there."

Giving away a teenager's social calendar is just as taboo as giving away a free name. You've got to be noncommittal. "Stephen will be sorry he missed you" is okay. Ditto, "Jane was talking about a movie, but she may have changed her mind," a statement that gives her lots of leeway and will not stand up in a court of law.

On the other hand, a teenager expects his or her father to pump as much information out of a caller as possible.

The absolute minimum is (a) who is calling, (b) the time of the call, (c) where the caller can be reached and (d) the sex of the caller.

You can forget about (a), (b) and (c), but heaven help you if you flub (d).

Establishing the sex of the caller is absolutely vital and any father who misses out on that one is definitely in trouble. Unfortunately, when your teenagers have friends whose voices haven't changed yet, it isn't easy.

Other things a teenager expects a father to learn are:

Was the call (in your opinion) to invite said teenaged son or daughter to a party, school dance, etc., or did the caller sound like someone who only wanted the title of the book required for the French course.

As a guess (in the case of a call for a teenaged daughter) would you say the caller was probably tall with a clear complexion?

Why do you think the caller didn't leave a number and, in your estimation, do you think he/she will call back if said teenager sits by the telephone for an hour or so?

The pressure of being the father of a teenager is enormous when the phone rings and sometimes you just want to let it ring rather than risk making a mistake.

Fortunately, with teenagers in the house you know one thing, the call is never for you.

LOATHE AT FIRST SIGHT

Ellen   Conford

Y ou are dripping on my toes."

"I'm sorry. I was admiring you from afar, and I wanted to admire you from a-near. From afar you looked terrific."

"Oh, thanks a lot. Meaning, up close I look like a toad."

"That's not what I meant at all! You look good up close, too. I love your bathing suit."

"Then why do you keep staring at my toes?"

"It's that stuff you've got on them. What do you call that?"

"Nail polish."

"I know, I know. I meant, what colour is it?"

"Rosy Dawn. Look, what is this with my toes?"

"Rosy Dawn. That's kind of romantic. I would have thought it was just pink."

"Will you stop talking about my toes? What are you, weird or something?"

"No! Oh, boy, this whole conversation has gotten off on the wrong foot. Wrong foot—ha! Get it? Foot, toes?"

"Ha ha."

"Just a little humour to lighten up a tense situation. I thought you'd appreciate a good joke."

"I do appreciate a *good* joke."

"I just thought it was too early in our relationship to make personal comments about how great you look in a bathing suit."

"Our relationship? *What* relationship?"

"The one we're going to have."

"Oh, really? Have you always been this unsure of yourself?"

"Have you always been this sarcastic? Look, I just wanted—"

"And besides, toes are personal. Personal comments about toes are just as—as personal as comments about how I look in a bathing suit."

"Well, all right, do you want me to tell you how I think you look in your bathing suit?"

"No. I'm really not interested in your opinion of how I look in my bathing suit."

"Okay, then. How do I look in mine?"

"Wet."

"Picture me dry."

"Please. I already had a nightmare last night."

"That's not very nice."

"Look, I'm sorry, but you just walk up to me, drip on my feet, and start raving about my toes and have the gall to make this incredible assumption that I'm going to be so devastated by your wit and charm—"

"And my good looks."

"—and your *modesty,* that I'll fall madly in love with you."

"Well, actually, I didn't expect you to fall madly in love with me in the first five minutes of our relationship."

"See, that's just what I mean! We don't have a relationship."

"I'm working on it. How'm I doing so far? Say, on a scale of one to ten."

"Minus three. Look, would you please move? You're standing in front of the sun and I'm going to have a big white stripe right in the middle of my back."

"Okay."

"I didn't mean for you to sit down. I meant for you to go away."

"But you didn't get a good look at me yet. All you could see when I was standing up was my knees. They're not necessarily my best feature. This way, you can look straight at me."

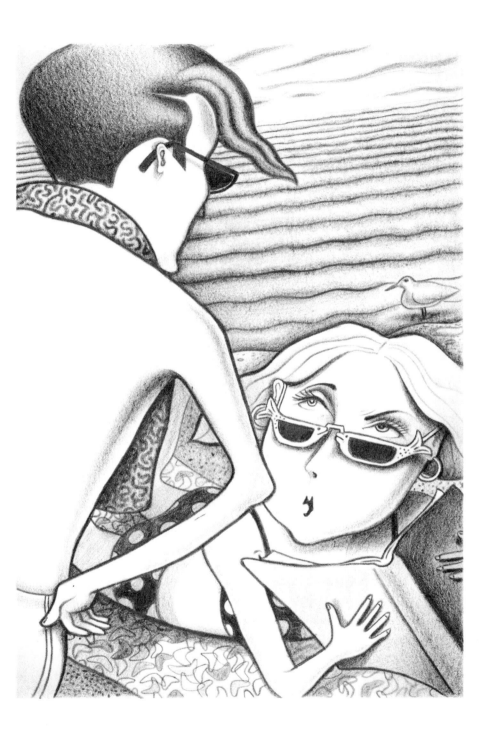

"Goody."

"Now, come on. I'm really pretty nice-looking."

"You're really pretty conceited."

"I'm just repeating what other people have told me. Some people think I look a lot like Burt Reynolds."

"Some people think the earth is flat."

"I'm getting this definite impression that you're not being dazzled by my wit and charm."

"How very observant of you."

"That's the first nice thing you've said to me."

"I was being sarcastic."

"I know, but I'm grasping at straws. I thought for sure if the wit and charm didn't work, I could always fall back on my good looks."

"You can fall back on your head, for all I care."

"This isn't going exactly as I planned it. Could we start all over again? Hi, there, my name's Alan. What's yours?"

"Hepzibah."

"...Hepzibah?...I see. And what do your friends call you?"

"Hepzibah."

"Uh, I don't want to insult you or anything, just in case your name really is Hepzibah, but I have this funny suspicion you're putting me on."

"Flurge."

"I beg your pardon?"

"My last name. Flurge."

"Hepzibah Flurge?"

"Right."

"You're going to burst out laughing any minute, I can tell. Come on, look me straight in the eye and tell me your name is Hepzibah Flurge."

"My name is Hep—Hep—"

"I knew it! You can't even keep a straight face. You can't even say it.... You know, you have beautiful eyes. What colour are they, exactly?"

"Brown."

"I know, but there are little specks of something in them that—"

"Probably sand."

"Now, come on, don't go all cold and sarcastic on me again. We were doing so well a minute ago."

"I hadn't noticed."

"Sure, you were laughing and everything. Really sort of loosening up, know what I mean? You were right here; you wouldn't have missed it. What's your name, really?"

"Anne."

"There, that's better. Mine's Alan."

"You told me."

"I know, but I'm running out of ideas. I did all my best stuff already."

"That was your best stuff? You're in trouble."

"Well, help me out. What kind of a person are you to leave me floundering around for something to say like this? I mean, this is really embarrassing. The least you could do is hold you up your end of the discussion."

"I didn't start this ridiculous conversation—if you can even call it a conversation. I don't see why I have to take any responsibility for keeping it up."

"What kind of an attitude is that? What if everybody felt that way? What kind of a world would this be?"

"Quiet."

"Boring."

"Peaceful."

"Not necessarily. If nobody communicated with anybody else there'd be wars all the time."

"There *are* wars all the time."

"…Uh, yeah. Well. Good point. Would you—um—like me to rub some suntan oil on your shoulders?"

"No, thank you."

"Would you like to rub some on mine?"

"Not particularly."

"Look, Anne, I'm getting desperate here. Where did I go wrong? Did I come on too strong?"

"Yes."

"A little heavy on the wit and charm?"

"Hey, I like wit and charm as much as the next person, but—"

"I overdid it."

"Yes."

"It was the toes, wasn't it? I really turned you off with that stuff about your toes."

"Yes."

"It was just what you call a conversational gambit. You know, an ice-breaker. I mean, not that I don't think your toes are extremely attractive—"

"*Alan*—"

"All right, all right, I swear I'll never mention your toes again. From this minute on, as far as I'm concerned, your toes don't exist. It's just—well, what *should* I have said?"

"What's wrong with hello?"

"Hello? Just hello? But what about after that? What happens after I say hello?"

"Who knows? If you don't try it you'll never find out."

"All right. Here goes. But I don't think this is going to work...Hello, Anne."

"Hello, Alan. How's the water?"

"Uh, it's very cold when you first go in, but it warms up after a while."

"A lot of things are like that, don't you think so, Alan?"

"I...I think I see what you mean."

"I felt certain you would..."

THE PRINCESS AND THE ZUCCHINI

A u d r e y   T h o m a s

This is the way it happened:
There had been a long, hot summer and the Royal Garden
was full to overflowing. The gardeners were hot and
grumpy and said they could not keep up with all the picking.
Everybody was hot and grumpy, even the King, even the Queen
and especially Princess Zona, who stood now, in her long white
night-dress, gazing down at the garden below her, glowing silver
in the moonlight. She hadn't been able to sleep at all, because of
the heat, and wished with all her heart for a thunderstorm and a
downpour to break the pressure of the night. It had not rained in
weeks and except for the garden, which was watered carefully
every evening as soon as the sun had left it, the rest of the royal
estate was parched and brown.

The garden looked inviting; she wanted to walk in the
garden with bare feet. She opened the door quietly and tiptoed
past the bedroom of her sleeping parents, tiptoed to the royal
staircase, and went quietly and carefully down, down, down, then
along corridors and passages, the moonlight streaming in through
leaded windows, until she reached the kitchen, then the pantry,
then the back door. The door creaked a little when she opened it
and she heard a mouse jump in one of the cupboards. Then she
was out, running across the dry lawn, which tickled her feet, and

through the white gate into the garden. The paths were cool and moist; the air was fragrant; her long blonde hair glittered and gleamed in the moonlight. It was very still.

"I could sleep out here," she thought. "I could get one of the gardeners to sling me up a hammock. I wish I'd thought of it sooner." She didn't want to go back up to her hot stuffy little room, pretty as it was. She wished, at least, that she had brought something to sit on.

And then, because she wasn't really paying attention, she tripped and stubbed her toe on a large zucchini.

"Thank God," a deep voice said. The princess froze in fear.

"Who's there?" she whispered, trembling. "What do you want?"

"Here," the voice said. It came from beside her and below.

"Where?" She thought of all the old stories of dwarfs and elves and gnomes. There must be a dwarf hiding in the vines. Her curiosity got the better of her fear.

"Come out where I can see you," she said. "It's so over-grown in here, I can't really see you at all."

"You're looking right at me," the deep voice said.

"I'm sorry. I may be looking right at you, but I still can't see you. Are you invisible or something?"

There was a deep, green groan.

"Would that it were that simple," the voice sighed. "I'm the zucchini you just stubbed your toe against."

"Don't be ridiculous."

"It's true."

"I'm not in the mood for jokes," she said, and drawing herself up to her full height of one hundred fifty centimetres and mustering all the dignity she could muster, standing there in her summer nightie, she demanded:

"Come out of there right now!"

"I wish I could," said the voice. "If you would kiss me, then I could."

"How can I kiss you when I don't know where you are?"

"I told you, I'm the zucchini."

"Are you a ventriloquist?" she said. "Are you a shape-shifter?"

"Neither of those," said the voice. "I'm a handsome young prince who has been cast under a wicked, wicked spell."

The princess laughed merrily; the laugh sounded like the tinkle of crystal chandeliers. She clapped her hands.

"I understand it all now. This is just one of those crazy

dreams I have sometimes. Like the time I dreamt I had a conversation with my horse. Or the time I dreamt I was a mermaid living underneath the sea. When I wake up tomorrow, I'll tell Mother. She always asks about my dreams."

"If you think this is a dream, why don't you try and wake yourself up?"

"That's true. I usually can, when I realize I'm dreaming." She shut her eyes tight and willed herself awake.

"It won't work, will it?" said the zucchini.

It wouldn't work. When she opened her eyes, she was not lying in her own little brass bed but was standing upright in the midnight garden.

"There's some mistake. This has to be a dream."

"A nightmare for me, maybe," said the voice, "but not a dream for you."

"Whoever heard of a prince being turned into a zucchini! A bear, yes; a swan, certainly; even a frog, although personally I find that one a little hard to swallow. But a vegetable! That's utterly ridiculous. Somebody's pulling my leg."

"Nobody's pulling your leg. I was standing in this garden one night, very late, gazing up at the light in your little window, trying to get up enough nerve to sing you a song I'd composed about your beauty, when all of a sudden I felt very strange, as though I'd faint if I didn't lie down; so I did that and the next thing I knew I was a tiny zucchini."

The princess laughed and laughed.

"You're not tiny now!"

"No. I grow bigger and bigger every day. It's all this watering and sunlight. I'm afraid I may burst."

"What makes you so sure that if I kiss you, you'll turn back into a prince?"

"Isn't your name Zona?"

"Yes it is. But I didn't choose it. It's a family name. The women in our family have always been called Zona. God knows why. I don't like it. As soon as I'm of age, I'm going to change it to Suzanne."

"I think it's a lovely name," the zucchini said. "I come from a land far away across the sea and I heard your name, fell in love with your name, long before I saw your portrait. I travelled for a year and a day to get here, saying your name softly to myself as I went, weary and wind-lashed, 'Zona, Zona, Zona,' to keep my courage up."

"But why does that convince you that I can save you? Love doesn't really conquer all and, even if it did, I'm not in love with you, it's the other way around."

"Don't you see? I've been changed into something beginning with the letter Z. Your name begins with Z. It must be a sign. I'm sure that only someone whose name begins with Z can save me."

"And if it's me and if my kiss can save you, what then?"

"What then! You know what then. 'Happily ever after.' "

"I don't think I could stand the idea of kissing a zucchini— it's so bizarre. What if somebody saw me!"

"Think about it for a while, but hurry."

"I am thinking about it; the idea repulses me." Then she added, "I have to go in now, I'm getting sleepy."

"Oh please Zona," the zucchini cried. "Just one little kiss."

"I'll think about it. Anyway, I'll come see you tomorrow night."

"I may have burst by then," he said sadly.

"Oh, I don't think so. And if you do, it will prove you're not really a prince, won't it?"

"How cruel you are!" he murmured.

"Just practical," she replied, and ran back the way she had come.

The next morning it all seemed like a very silly dream. Nevertheless, she went out right after breakfast and stuck a little hand-lettered sign in front of the zucchini. "PLEASE DON'T PICK THIS ZUCCHINI" it said. "BY ORDER OF H.R.H. PRINCESS ZONA." She had lessons to do, so she didn't stop to chat, just stuck a broken bean pole through the sign and pushed it into the moist earth near the vine. "I'll come back tonight," she whispered, hoping none of the gardeners would overhear her.

It wasn't a dream. The zucchini really had talked to her, really had told her his sad tale of woe. Every evening, close to midnight, the young princess walked up and down between the bean rows, the ripe tomatoes, the broccoli and cucumbers until she reached the back of the garden where the zucchinis grew. There she sat on a cushion and listened to stories of life in the distant land from which the prince—if he was a prince—had come. He had a deep, thrilling voice and she came to look forward eagerly to his accounts of his adventures.

But she would not kiss him; she absolutely refused.

"Have you no pity?" he cried. "Have you no heart?"

"I don't quite understand it myself," she admitted. "Something keeps holding me back. At the risk of sounding offensive, I think it really does have to do with the fact that you are a zucchini. What kind of spell is that? There's something not quite noble about it somehow."

He laughed bitterly. "Do you think the Frog Prince found it 'noble' to be a frog?"

"I suppose he didn't. But that's another story and another princess; it's nothing to do with me." She sighed. "Since you had to go through all this—and I still don't understand who could have done it to you—why couldn't you have been changed into an eagle, or a swan, or a chestnut stallion?"

"Well I wasn't. I was standing in a vegetable garden and I was changed into a garden vegetable. That's just the way it was."

"Well it's too bad you weren't standing by the peacocks or at the stable door."

"Ha ha." He paused. "Sometimes you're not very nice to me, you know. I suffer horribly."

"How can I be nice to you when 'you' is only a voice? I must admit, however, that the voice is very beautiful."

"Doesn't it make you want to see the rest?"

"Yes, no, oh—I don't know! Don't rush me."

"I can't get much bigger, Zona. I feel that if you don't release me, then I'll die."

"Tell me again about the 'Happily ever after.'"

The rains had still not come and everyone seemed to exist in a kind of terrible tension. The King snapped at the Queen, the Queen snapped at Zona, Zona snapped at everybody. One night she sat at her dressing table brushing her long golden hair and thinking. She tried to imagine the young prince before he had been changed into a zucchini. She tried to imagine happily ever after.

"Ninety-eight—ninety-nine—one hundred," she said, and put down the hairbrush. She stared at herself in the mirror. The zucchini had told her she was the most beautiful girl he had ever seen. Her mother and father told her she was beautiful. Her mirror said the same thing.

"But who is the 'I' who is so beautiful," she thought.

"Who is she? I will be fifteen next month. That's a lot of Ever After."

She sat in her night-dress, with her hands in her lap. long after her candle had sputtered and gone out. She sat like that, in the darkness, far into the night.

It had finally rained, and the King and Queen and Princess Zona were smiling as they dined *en famille* and listened to the blessed sound of the rain on the castle roof. It was the cook's day off and Zona had begged her mother to let her prepare the evening meal.

"Absolutely delicious," said the King, wiping his bowl with a piece of bread. "What did you say it was again?"

"Ratatouille," Zona said. "I found the recipe in *The Joy of Cooking.*"

"It really is very very good, dear," said the Queen. "We'll have to have it again."

The King and Queen smiled at one another tenderly.

"Our little girl is growing up," said the King.

"It won't be long," said the Queen, "before she'll be having boyfriends."

Zona smiled at them both and offered the dish around a second time.

No one is immune to sorrow. Sadness can come at any tim

and for many reasons. The way we deal with it can teach u

a lot about ourselves and others, and what it means

to be human.

FOUR GENERATIONS

J o y c e M a y n a r d

My mother called last week to tell me that my grandmother is dying. She has refused an operation that would postpone, but not prevent, her death from pancreatic cancer. She can't eat, she has been hemorrhaging, and she has severe jaundice. "I always prided myself on being different," she told my mother. "Now I am different. I'm yellow."

My mother, telling me this news, began to cry. So I became the mother for a moment, reminding her, reasonably, that my grandmother is eighty-seven, she's had a full life, she has all her faculties, and no one who knows her could wish that she live long enough to lose them. Lately my mother has been finding notes in my grandmother's drawers at the nursing home, reminding her, "Joyce's husband's name is Steve. Their daughter is Audrey." In the last few years she hadn't had the strength to cook or garden, and she's begun to say she's had enough of living.

My grandmother was born in Russia, in 1892—the eldest daughter in a large and prosperous Jewish family. But the prosperity didn't last. She tells stories of the pogroms and the cossacks who raped her when she was twelve. Soon after that, her family emigrated to Canada, where she met my grandfather.

Their children were the centre of their life. The story I loved best, as a child, was of my grandfather opening every box of Cracker Jack in the general store he ran, in search of the particular tin toy my mother coveted. Though they never had much money, my grandmother saw to it that her daughter had elocution lessons and piano lessons, and assured her that she would go to college.

But while she was at college, my mother met my father, who was blue-eyed and blond-haired and not Jewish. When my father sent love letters to my mother, my grandmother would open and hide them, and when my mother told her parents she was going to marry this man, my grandmother said if that happened, it would kill her.

Not likely, of course. My grandmother is a woman who used to crack Brazil nuts open with her teeth, a woman who once lifted a car off the ground, when there was an accident and it had to be moved. She has been representing her death as imminent ever since I've known her—twenty-five years—and has discussed, at length, the distribution of her possessions and her lamb coat. Every time we said goodbye, after our annual visit to Winnipeg, she'd weep and say she'd never see us again. But in the meantime, while every other relative of her generation, and a good many of the younger ones, has died (nursed usually by her), she has kept making knishes, shopping for bargains, tending the healthiest plants I've ever seen.

After my grandfather died, my grandmother lived, more than ever, through her children. When she came to visit, I would hide my diary. She couldn't understand any desire for privacy. She couldn't bear it if my mother left the house without her.

This possessiveness is what made my mother furious (and then guilt-ridden that she felt that way, when of course she owed so much to her mother). So I harboured the resentment that my mother—and dutiful daughter—would not allow herself. I—who had always performed specially well for my grandmother, danced and sung for her, presented her with kisses and good report cards—stopped writing to her, ceased to visit.

But when I heard that she was dying, I realized I wanted to go to Winnipeg to see her one more time. Mostly to make my mother happy, I told myself (certain patterns being hard to break). But also, I was offering up one more particularly fine accomplishment: my own dark-eyed, dark-skinned, dark-haired daughter, whom my grandmother had never met.

I put on my daughter's best dress for our visit to Winnipeg, the way the best dresses were always put on me, and I filled my pockets with animal crackers, in case Audrey started to cry. I scrubbed her face mercilessly. On the elevator going up to her room, I realized how much I was sweating.

Grandma was lying flat with an IV tube in her arm and her eyes shut, but she opened them when I leaned over to kiss her. "It's Fredelle's daughter, Joyce," I yelled, because she doesn't hear well anymore, but I could see that no explanation was necessary. "You came," she said. "You brought the baby."

Audrey is just one, but she has seen enough of the world to know that people in beds are not meant to be so still and yellow, and she looked frightened. I had never wanted, more, for her to smile.

Then Grandma waved at her—the same kind of slow, finger-flexing wave a baby makes—and Audrey waved back. I spread her toys out on my grandmother's bed and sat her down. There she stayed, most of the afternoon, playing and humming and sipping on her bottle, taking a nap at one point, leaning against my grandmother's leg. When I cranked her Snoopy guitar, Audrey stood up on the bed and danced. Grandma wouldn't talk much anymore, though every once in a while she would say how sorry she was that she wasn't having a better day. "I'm not always like this," she said.

Mostly she just watched Audrey. Sometimes Audrey would get off the bed, inspect the get-well cards, totter down the hall. "Where is she?" Grandma kept asking. "Who's looking after her?" I had the feeling, even then, that if I'd said, "Audrey's lighting matches," Grandma would have shot up to rescue her.

We were flying home that night, and I had dreaded telling her, remembering all those other tearful partings. But in the end, I was the one who cried. She had said she was ready to die. But as I leaned over to stroke her forehead, what she said was, "I wish I had your hair" and "I wish I was well."

On the plane flying home, with Audrey in my arms, I thought about mothers and daughters, and the four generations of the family that I know most intimately. Every one of those mothers loves and needs her daughter more than her daughter will love or need her some day, and we are, each of us, the only person on earth who is quite so consumingly interested in our child.

Sometimes I kiss and hug Audrey so much she starts crying—which is, in effect, what my grandmother was doing to my mother, all her life. And what makes my mother grieve right now, I think, is not simply that her mother will die in a day or two, but that, once her mother dies, there will never again be someone to love her in quite such an unreserved, unquestioning way. No one else who believes that, fifty years ago, she could have put Shirley Temple out of a job, no one else who remembers the moment of her birth. She will only be a mother, then, not a daughter anymore.

Audrey and I have stopped over for a night in Toronto, where my mother lives. Tomorrow she will go to a safe-deposit box at the bank and take out the receipt for my grandmother's burial plot. Then she will fly back to Winnipeg, where, for the first time in anybody's memory, there was waist-high snow on April Fool's Day. But tonight she is feeding me, as she always does when I come, and I am eating more than I do anywhere else. I admire the wedding china (once my grandmother's) that my mother has set on the table. She says (the way Grandma used to say to her, of the lamb coat), "Some day it will be yours."

DAY OF THE BUTTERFLY

A l i c e   M u n r o

I do not remember when Myra Sayla came to town, though she must have been in our class at school for two or three years. I start remembering her in the last year, when her little brother Jimmy Sayla was in Grade One. Jimmy Sayla was not used to going to the bathroom by himself and he would have to come to the Grade Six door and ask for Myra and she would take him downstairs. Quite often he would not get to Myra in time and there would be a big dark stain on his little button-on cotton pants. Then Myra had to come and ask the teacher: "Please may I take my brother home, he has wet himself?"

That was what she said the first time and everybody in the front seats heard her—though Myra's voice was the lightest singsong—and there was a muted giggling which alerted the rest of the class. Our teacher, a cold gentle girl who wore glasses with thin gold rims and in the stiff solicitude of certain poses resembled a giraffe, wrote something on a piece of paper and showed it to Myra. And Myra recited uncertainly: "My brother has had an accident, please, teacher."

Everybody knew of Jimmy Sayla's shame and at recess (if he was not being kept in, as he often was, for doing something he shouldn't in school) he did not dare go out on the school grounds, where the other little boys, and some bigger ones, were waiting to chase him and corner him against the back fence and thrash him with tree branches. He had to stay with Myra. But at our school there were the two sides, the Boys' Side and the Girls' Side, and it was believed that if you so much as stepped on the side that was not your own you might easily get the strap. Jimmy could not go out on the Girls' Side and Myra could not go out on the Boys' Side, and no one was allowed to stay in the school unless it was raining or snowing. So Myra and Jimmy spent every recess standing in the little back porch between the two sides. Perhaps they watched the baseball games, the tag and skipping and building of leaf houses in the fall and snow forts in the winter; perhaps they did not watch at all. Whenever you happened to look at them their heads were slightly bent, their narrow bodies hunched in, quite still. They had long smooth oval faces, melancholy and discreet—dark, oily, shining hair. The little boy's was long, clipped at home, and Myra's was worn in heavy braids coiled on top of her head so that she looked, from a distance, as if she was wearing a turban too big for her. Over their dark eyes the lids were never fully raised; they had a weary look. But it was more than that. They were like children in a medieval painting, they were like small figures carved of wood, for worship or magic, with faces smooth and aged, and meekly, cryptically uncommunicative.

Most of the teachers at our school had been teaching for a long time and at recess they would disappear into the teachers' room and not bother us. But our own teacher, the young woman of the fragile gold-rimmed glasses, was apt to watch us from a window and sometimes come out, looking brisk and uncomfortable, to stop a fight among the little girls or start a running game among the big ones, who had been huddled together playing Truth or Secrets. One day she came out and called, "Girls in Grade Six, I want to talk to you!" She smiled persuasively, earnestly, and with dreadful unease, showing fine gold rims around her teeth. She said, "There is a girl in Grade Six called Myra Sayla. She *is* in your grade, isn't she?"

We mumbled. But there was a coo from Gladys Healey. "Yes, Miss Darling!"

"Well, why is she never playing with the rest of you? Every day I see her standing in the back porch, never playing. Do you think she looks very happy standing back there? Do you think you would be very happy, if *you* were left back there?"

Nobody answered; we faced Miss Darling, all respectful, self-possessed, and bored with the unreality of her question. Then Gladys said, "Myra can't come out with us, Miss Darling. Myra has to look after her little brother!"

"Oh," said Miss Darling dubiously. "Well you ought to try to be nicer to her anyway. Don't you think so? Don't you? You will try to be nicer, won't you? I know you will." Poor Miss Darling! Her campaigns were soon confused, her persuasions turned to bleating and uncertain pleas.

When she had gone Gladys Healey said softly, "You will try to be nicer, won't you? I *know* you will!" and then drawing her lip back over her big teeth she yelled exuberantly, "I don't care if it rains or freezes." She went through the whole verse and ended it with a spectacular twirl of her Royal Stuart tartan skirt. Mr. Healey ran a Dry Goods and Ladies' Wear, and his daughter's leadership in our class was partly due to her flashing plaid skirts and organdy blouses and velvet jackets with brass buttons, but also to her early-maturing bust and the fine brutal force of her personality. Now we all began to imitate Miss Darling.

We had not paid much attention to Myra before this. But now a game was developed; it started with saying, "Let's be nice to Myra!" Then we would walk up to her in formal groups of three or four and at a signal, say together. "Hel-lo Myra, Hello *My*-ra!" and follow up with something like, "What do you wash your hair in, Myra, it's so nice and shiny, *My*-ra." "Oh she washes it in cod-liver oil, don't you, Myra, she washes it in cod-liver oil, can't you smell it?"

And to tell the truth there was a smell about Myra, but it was a rotten-sweetish smell as of bad fruit. That was what the Saylas did, kept a little fruit store. Her father sat all day on a stool by the window, with his shirt open over his swelling stomach and tufts of black hair showing around his belly button; he chewed garlic. But if you went into the store it was Mrs. Sayla who came to wait on you, appearing silently between the limp print curtains hung across the back of the store. Her hair was crimped in black waves and she smiled with her full lips held together, stretched as far as they would go; she told you the price in a little rapping voice, daring you to challenge her and, when you did not, handed you the bag of fruit with open mockery in her eyes.

One morning in the winter I was walking up the school hill very early; a neighbour had given me a ride into town. I lived about a kilometre out of town, on a farm, and I should not have been going to the town school at all, but to a country school nearby where there were half a dozen pupils and a teacher a little demented since her change of life. But my mother, who was an ambitious woman, had prevailed on the town trustees to accept me and my father to pay the extra tuition, and I went to school in town. I was the only one in the class who carried a lunch pail and ate peanut-butter sandwiches in the high, bare, mustard-coloured cloakroom, the only one who had to wear rubber boots in the spring, when the roads were heavy with mud. I felt a little danger, on account of this; but I could not tell exactly what it was.

I saw Myra and Jimmy ahead of me on the hill; they always went to school very early—sometimes so early that they had to stand outside waiting for the janitor to open the door. They were walking slowly, and now and then Myra half turned around. I had often loitered in that way, wanting to walk with some important girl who was behind me, and not quite daring to stop and wait. Now it occurred to me that Myra might be doing this with me. I did not know what to do. I could not afford to be seen walking with her, and I did not even want to—but, on the other hand, the flattery of those humble, hopeful turnings was not lost on me. A role was shaping for me that I could not resist playing. I felt a great pleasurable rush of self-conscious benevolence; before I thought what I was doing I called, "Myra! Hey, Myra, wait up, I got some Cracker Jack!" and I quickened my pace as she stopped.

Myra waited, but she did not look at me; she waited in the withdrawn and rigid attitude with which she always met us.

Perhaps she thought I was playing a trick on her, perhaps she expected me to run past and throw an empty Cracker Jack box in her face. And I opened the box and held it out to her. She took a little. Jimmy ducked behind her coat and would not take any when I offered the box to him.

"He's shy," I said reassuringly. "A lot of little kids are shy like that. He'll probably grow out of it."

"Yes," said Myra.

"I have a brother four," I said. "He's awfully shy." He wasn't. "Have some more Cracker Jack," I said. "I used to eat Cracker Jack all the time but I don't any more. I think it's bad for your complexion."

There was a silence.

"Do you like Art?" said Myra faintly.

"No. I like Social Studies and Spelling and Health."

"I like Art and Arithmetic." Myra could add and multiply in

her head faster than anyone else in the class.

"I wish I was as good as you. In Arithmetic," I said, and felt magnanimous.

"But I am no good at Spelling," said Myra. "I make the most mistakes, I'll fail maybe." She did not sound unhappy about this, but pleased to have such a thing to say. She kept her head turned away from me staring at the dirty snowbanks along Victoria Street, and as she talked she made a sound as if she was wetting her lips with her tongue.

"You won't fail," I said. "You are too good in Arithmetic. What are you going to be when you grow up?"

She looked bewildered. "I will help my mother," she said. "And work in the store."

"Well, I am going to be an airplane hostess," I said. "But don't mention it to anybody. I haven't told many people."

"No, I won't," said Myra. "Do you read Steve Canyon in the paper?"

"Yes." It was queer to think that Myra, too, read the comics, or that she did anything at all, apart from her role at the school. "Do you read Rip Kirby?"

"Do you read Orphan Annie?"

"Do you read Betsy and The Boys?"

"You haven't had hardly any Cracker Jack," I said. "Have some. Take a whole handful."

Myra looked into the box. "There's a prize in there," she said. She pulled it out. It was a brooch, a little tin butterfly, painted gold with bits of coloured glass stuck onto it to look like jewels. She held it in her brown hand, smiling slightly.

I said, "Do you like that?"

Myra said, "I like them blue stones. Blue stones are sapphires."

"I know. My birthstone is sapphire. What is your birthstone?"

"I don't know."

"When is your birthday?"

"July."

172

"Then yours is ruby."

"I like sapphire better," said Myra. "I like yours." She handed me the brooch.

"You keep it," I said. "Finders keepers."

Myra kept holding it out, as if she did not know what I meant. "Finders keepers," I said.

"It was your Cracker Jack," said Myra, scared and solemn. "You bought it."

"Well you found it."

"No—" said Myra.

"Go on!" I said. "Here, I'll *give* it to you." I took the brooch from her and pushed it back into her hand.

We were both surprised. We looked at each other; I flushed but Myra did not. I realized the pledge as our fingers touched; I was panicky, but *all right*. I thought, I can come early and walk with her other mornings. I can go and talk to her at recess. Why not? *Why not?*

Myra put the brooch in her pocket. She said, "I can wear it on my good dress. My good dress is blue."

I knew it would be. Myra wore out her good dresses at school. Even in midwinter among the plaid wool skirts and serge tunics, she glimmered sadly in sky-blue taffeta, in dusty turquoise crepe, a grown woman's dress made over, weighted by a big bow at the vee of the neck and folding empty over Myra's narrow chest.

And I was glad she had not put it on. If someone asked her where she got it, and she told them, what would I say?

It was the day after this, or the week after, that Myra did not come to school. Often she was kept at home to help. But this time she did not come back. For a week, then two weeks, her desk was empty. Then we had a moving day at school and Myra's books were taken out of her desk and put on a shelf in the closet. Miss Darling said, "We'll find a seat when she comes back." And she stopped calling Myra's name when she took attendance.

Jimmy Sayla did not come to school either, having no one to take him to the bathroom.

In the fourth week or the fifth, that Myra had been away, Gladys Healey came to school and said, "Do you know what—Myra Sayla is sick in the hospital."

It was true. Gladys Healey had an aunt who was a nurse. Gladys put up her hand in the middle of Spelling and told Miss Darling. "I thought you might like to know," she said. "Oh yes," said Miss Darling. "I do know."

"What has she got?" we said to Gladys.

And Gladys said, "Akemia, or something. And she has blood transfusions." She said to Miss Darling, "My aunt is a nurse."

So Miss Darling had the whole class write Myra a letter, in which everybody said, "Dear Myra, We are all writing you a letter. We hope you will soon be better and be back to school, Yours truly..." And Miss Darling said, "I've thought of something. Who would like to go up to the hospital and visit Myra on the twentieth of March, for a birthday party?"

I said, "Her birthday's in July."

"I know," said Miss Darling. "It's the twentieth of July. So this year she could have it on the twentieth of March, because she's sick."

"But her *birthday* is in July."

"Because she's sick," said Miss Darling, with a warning shrillness. "The cook at the hospital would make a cake and you could all give a little present, twenty-five cents or so. It would have to be between two and four, because that's visiting hours. And we couldn't all go, it'd be too many. So who wants to go and who wants to stay here and do supplementary reading?"

We all put up our hands. Miss Darling got out the spelling records and picked out the first fifteen, twelve girls and three boys. Then the three boys did not want to go so she picked out the next three girls. And I do not know when it was, but I think it was probably at this moment that the birthday party of Myra Sayla became fashionable.

Perhaps it was because Gladys Healey had an aunt who was a nurse, perhaps it was the excitement of sickness and hospitals, or simply the fact that Myra was so entirely, impressively set free of all the rules and conditions of our lives. We began to talk of her as if she were something we owned, and her party became a cause; with womanly heaviness we discussed it at recess, and decided that twenty-five cents was too low.

We all went up to the hospital on a sunny afternoon when the snow was melting, carrying our presents, and a nurse led us upstairs, single file, and down a hall past half-closed doors and dim conversations. She and Miss Darling kept saying, "Sh-Sh," but we were going on tiptoe anyway; our hospital demeanour was perfect.

At this small country hospital there was no children's ward, and Myra was not really a child; they had put her in with two old women. A nurse was putting screens around them as we came in.

Myra was sitting up in bed, in a bulky stiff hospital gown. Her hair was down, the long braids falling over her shoulders and down the coverlet. But her face was the same, always the same.

She had been told something about the party, Miss Darling said, so the surprise would not upset her; but it seemed she had not believed, or had not understood what it was. She watched us as she used to watch in the school grounds when we played.

"Well, here we are!" said Miss Darling. "Here we are!"

And we said, "Happy birthday, Myra! Hello, Myra, happy birthday!" Myra said, "My birthday is in July." Her voice was lighter than ever, drifting, expressionless.

"Never mind when it is, really," said Miss Darling. "Pretend it's now! How old are you, Myra?"

"Eleven," Myra said. "In July."

Then we all took off our coats and emerged in our party dresses, and laid our presents, in their pale flowery wrappings on Myra's bed. Some of our mothers had made immense, complicated bows of fine satin ribbon, some of them had even taped on little bouquets of imitation roses and lilies of the valley. "Here Myra," we said, "here Myra, happy birthday." Myra did not look at us, but at the ribbons, pink and blue and speckled with silver, and the miniature bouquets; they pleased her, as the butterfly had done. An innocent look came into her face, a partial, private smile.

"Open them, Myra," said Miss Darling. "They're for you!"

Myra gathered the presents around her, fingering them, with this smile, and a cautious realization, an unexpected pride. She said, "Saturday I'm going to London to St. Joseph's Hospital."

"That's where my mother was at," somebody said. "We went and saw her. They've got all nuns there."

"My father's sister is a nun," said Myra calmly.

She began to unwrap the presents, with an air that not even Gladys could have bettered, folding the tissue paper and the ribbons, and drawing out books and puzzles and cutouts as if they were all prizes she had won. Miss Darling said that maybe she should say thank you, and the person's name with every gift she opened, to make sure she knew whom it was from, and so Myra said, "Thank you, Mary Louise, thank you, Carol," and when she came to mine she said, "Thank you, Helen." Everyone explained their presents to her and there was talking and excitement and a little gaiety, which Myra presided over, though she was not gay. A cake was brought in with *Happy Birthday Myra* written on it, pink on white, and eleven candles. Miss Darling lit the candles and we all sang "Happy Birthday to You," and cried, "Make a wish, Myra, make a wish—" and Myra blew them out. Then we all had cake and strawberry ice cream.

At four o'clock a buzzer sounded and the nurse took out what was left of the cake, and the dirty dishes, and we put on our coats to go home. Everybody said, "Goodbye, Myra," and Myra sat in the bed watching us go, her back straight, not supported by any pillow, her hands resting on the gifts. But at the door I heard her call; she called "Helen!" Only a couple of the others heard; Miss Darling did not hear, she had gone out ahead. I went back to the bed.

Myra said, "I got too many things. You take something."

"What?" I said, "It's for your birthday. You always get a lot at a birthday."

"Well you take something," Myra said. She picked up a leatherette case with a mirror in it, a comb and a nail file and a natural lipstick and a small handkerchief edged with gold thread. I had noticed it before. "You take that," she said.

"Don't you want it?"

"You take it." She put it into my hand. Our fingers touched again.

"When I come back from London," Myra said, "you can come and play at my place after school."

"Okay," I said. Outside the hospital window there was a clear carrying sound of somebody playing in the street, maybe chasing with the last snowballs of the year. This sound made Myra, her triumph and her bounty, and most of her future in which she had found this place for me, turn shadowy, turn dark. All the presents on the bed, the folded paper and ribbons, those guilt-tinged offerings, had passed into this shadow, they were no longer innocent objects to be touched, exchanged, accepted without danger. I didn't want to take the case now but I could not think how to get out of it, what lie to tell. I'll give it away, I thought, I won't ever play with it. I would let my little brother pull it apart.

The nurse came back, carrying a glass of chocolate milk.

"What's the matter, didn't you hear the buzzer?"

So I was released, set free by the barriers which now closed about Myra, her unknown, exalted, ether-smelling hospital world, and by the treachery of my own heart. "Well, thank you," I said. "Thank you for the thing. Goodbye."

Did Myra ever say goodbye? Not likely. She sat in her high bed, her delicate brown neck, rising out of a hospital gown too big for her, her brown carved face immune to treachery, her offering perhaps already forgotten, prepared to be set apart for legendary uses, as she was even in the back porch at school.

THE COLT

Wallace Stegner

IT was the swift coming of spring that let things happen. It was spring, and the opening of the roads, that took his father out of town. It was spring that clogged the river with floodwater and ice pans, sent the dogs racing in wild aimless packs, ripped the railroad bridge out and scattered it down the river for exuberant townspeople to fish out piecemeal. It was spring that drove the whole town to the riverbank with pike-poles and coffeepots and boxes of sandwiches for an impromptu picnic, lifting their sober responsibilities out of them and making them whoop blessings on the Canadian Pacific Railroad for a winter's firewood. Nothing might have gone wrong except for the coming of spring. Some of the neighbours might have noticed and let them know; Bruce might not have forgotten; his mother might have remembered and sent him out again after dark.

But the spring came, and the ice went out, and that night Bruce went to bed drunk and exhausted with excitement. In the restless sleep just before waking he dreamed of wolves and wild hunts, but when he awoke finally he realized that he had not been dreaming the noise. The window, wide open for the first time in months, let in a shivery draught of fresh, damp air, and he heard the faint yelping far down in the bend of the river.

He dressed and went downstairs, crowding his bottom into

the warm oven, not because he was cold but because it had been a ritual for so long that not even the sight of the sun outside could convince him it wasn't necessary. The dogs were still yapping; he heard them through the open door.

"What's the matter with all the pooches?" he said. "Where's Spot?"

"He's out with them," his mother said. "They've probably got a porcupine treed. Dogs go crazy in the spring."

"It's dog days they go crazy."

"They go crazy in the spring, too." She hummed a little as she set the table. "You'd better go feed the horses. Breakfast won't be for ten minutes. And see if Daisy is all right."

Bruce stood perfectly still in the middle of the kitchen. "Oh my gosh!" he said. "I left Daisy picketed out all night!"

His mother's head jerked around. "Where?"

"Down in the bend."

"Where those dogs are?"

"Yes," he said, sick and afraid. "Maybe she's had her colt."

"She shouldn't for two or three days," his mother said. But just looking at her he knew that it might be bad, that there was something to be afraid of. In another moment they were both out the door, both running.

But it couldn't be Daisy they were barking at, he thought as he raced around Chance's barn. He'd picketed her higher up, not clear down in the U where the dogs were. His eyes swept the brown, wet, close-cropped meadow, the edge of the brush where the river ran close under the north bench. The mare wasn't there! He opened his mouth and half turned, running, to shout at his mother coming behind him, and then sprinted for the deep curve of the bend.

As soon as he rounded the little clump of brush that fringed the cutbank behind Chance's he saw them. The mare stood planted, a bay spot against the gray brush, and in front of her, on the ground, was another smaller spot. Six or eight dogs were leaping around, barking, sitting. Even at that distance he recognized Spot and the Chapmans' Airedale.

He shouted and pumped on. At a gravelly patch he stooped and clawed and straightened, still running, with a handful of pebbles. In one pausing, straddling, aiming motion he left fly a rock at the distant pack. It fell far short, but they turned their heads, sat on their haunches and let out defiant short barks. Their tongues lolled as if they had run far.

Bruce yelled and threw again, one eye on the dogs and the other on the chestnut colt in front of the mare's feet. The mare's ears were back, and as he ran Bruce saw the colt's head bob up and down. It was all right then. The colt was alive. He slowed and came up quietly. Never move fast or speak loud around an animal, Pa said.

The colt struggled again, raised its head with white eyeballs rolling, spraddled its white-stockinged legs and tried to stand. "Easy, boy," Bruce said. "Take it easy, old fella." His mother arrived, getting her breath, her hair half down, and he turned to her gleefully. "It's all right, Ma. They didn't hurt anything. Isn't he a beauty, Ma?"

He stroked Daisy's nose. She was heaving, her ears pricking forward and back; her flanks were lathered, and she trembled. Patting her gently, he watched the colt, sitting now like a dog on its haunches, and his happiness that nothing had really been hurt bubbled out of him. "Lookit, Ma," he said. "He's got four white socks. Can I call him Socks, Ma? He sure is a nice colt, isn't he? Aren't you Socks, old boy?" He reached down to touch the chestnut's forelock, and the colt struggled, pulling away.

Then Bruce saw his mother's face. It was quiet, too quiet. She hadn't answered a word to all his jabber. Instead she knelt down, about three metres from the squatting colt, and stared at it. The boy's eyes followed hers. There was something funny about...

"Ma!" he said. "What's the matter with its front feet?"

He left Daisy's head and came around, staring. The colt's pasterns looked bent—*were* bent, so that they flattened clear to the ground under its weight. Frightened by Bruce's movement, the chestnut flopped and floundered to its feet, pressing close to its mother. And it walked, Bruce saw, flat on its fetlocks, its hooves sticking out in front like a movie comedian's too-large shoes.

Bruce's mother pressed her lips together, shaking her head. She moved so gently that she got her hand on the colt's poll, and he bobbed against the pleasant scratching. "You poor broken-legged thing," she said with tears in her eyes. "You poor little friendly ruined thing!"

Still quietly, she turned toward the dogs, and for the first time in his life Bruce heard her curse. Quietly, almost in a whisper, she cursed them as they sat with hanging tongues just out of reach. "Damn you," she said. "Damn your wild hearts, chasing a mother and a poor little colt."

To Bruce, standing with trembling lip, she said, "Go get Jim Enich. Tell him to bring a wagon. And don't cry. It's not your fault."

His mouth tightened, a sob jerked in his chest. He bit his lip and drew his face down tight to keep from crying, but his eyes filled and ran over.

"It is too my fault!" he said, and turned and ran.

Later, as they came in the wagon up along the cutbank, the colt tied down in the wagon box with his head sometimes lifting, sometimes bumping on the boards, the mare trotting after with chuckling vibrations of solicitude in her throat, Bruce leaned far over and tried to touch the colt's haunch. "Gee!" he said. "Poor old Socks."

His mother's arm was around him, keeping him from leaning over too far. He didn't watch where they were until he heard his mother say in surprise and relief, "Why, there's Pa!"

Instantly he was terrified. He had forgotten and left Daisy staked out all night. It was his fault, the whole thing. He slid back into the seat and crouched between Enich and his mother, watching from that narrow space like a gopher from its hole. He saw the Ford against the barn and his father's big body leaning into it pulling out gunny sacks and straw. There was mud all over the car, mud on his father's pants. He crouched deeper into his crevice and watched his father's face while his mother was telling what had happened.

Then Pa and Jim Enich lifted and slid the colt down to the ground, and Pa stooped to feel its fetlocks. His face was still, red from windburn, and his big square hands were muddy. After a long examination he straightened up.

"Would've been a nice colt," he said. "Damn a pack of mangy mongrels, anyway." He brushed his pants and looked at Bruce's mother. "How come Daisy was out?"

"I told Bruce to take her out. The barn seems so cramped for her, and I thought it would do her good to stretch her legs. And then the ice went out, and the bridge with it, and there was a lot of excitement...." She spoke very fast, and in her voice Bruce heard the echo of his own fear and guilt. She was trying to protect him, but in his mind he knew he was to blame.

"I didn't mean to leave her out, Pa," he said. His voice squeaked, and he swallowed. "I was going to bring her in before supper, only when the bridge..."

His father's somber eyes rested on him, and he stopped. But his father didn't fly into a rage. He just seemed tired. He looked at the colt and then at Enich. "Total loss?" he said.

Enich had a leathery, withered face, with two deep creases from beside his nose to the corner of his mouth. A brown mole hid in the left one, and it emerged and disappeared as he chewed a dry grass stem. "Hide," he said.

Bruce closed his dry mouth, swallowed. "Pa!" he said. "It won't have to be shot, will it?"

"What else can you do with it?" his father said. "A crippled horse is no good. It's just plain mercy to shoot it."

"Give it to me, Pa. I'll keep it lying down and heal it up."

"Yeah," his father said, without sarcasm and without mirth. "You could keep it lying down about one hour."

Bruce's mother came up next to him, as if the two of them were standing against the others. "Jim," she said quickly, "isn't there some kind of brace you could put on it? I remember my dad had a horse once that broke a leg below the knee, and he saved it that way."

"Not much chance," Enich said. "Both legs, like that." He picked a weed and stripped the dry branches from the stalk. "You can't make a horse understand he has to keep still."

"But wouldn't it be worth trying?" she said. "Children's bones heal so fast, I should think a colt's would too."

"I don't know. There's an outside chance, maybe."

"Bo," she said to her husband, "why don't we try it? It seems such a shame, a lovely colt like that."

"I know it's a shame!" he said. "I don't like shooting colts any better than you do. But I never saw a broken-legged colt get well. It'd just be a lot of worry and trouble, and then you'd have to shoot it finally anyway."

"Please," she said. She nodded at him slightly, and then the eyes of both were on Bruce. He felt the tears coming up again, and turned to grope for the colt's ears. It tried to struggle to its feet, and Enich put his foot on its neck. The mare chuckled anxiously.

"How much this hobble brace kind of thing cost?" the father said finally. Bruce turned again, his mouth open with hope.

"Two-three dollars, is all," Enich said.

"You think it's got a chance?"

"One in a thousand, maybe."

"All right. Let's go see MacDonald."

"Oh, good!" Bruce's mother said, and put her arm around him tight.

"I don't know whether it's good or not," the father said. "We might wish we never did it." To Bruce he said, "It's your responsibility. You got to take complete care of it."

"I will!" Bruce said. He took his hand out of his pocket and rubbed below his eye with his knuckles. "I'll take care of it every day."

Big with contrition and shame and gratitude and the sudden sense of immense responsibility, he watched his father and Enich start for the house to get a tape measure. When they were ten metres away he said loudly, "Thanks, Pa. Thanks an awful lot."

His father half turned, said something to Enich. Bruce stooped to stroke the colt, looked at his mother, started to laugh

184

and felt it turn horribly into a sob. When he turned away so that his mother wouldn't notice, he saw his dog Spot looking inquiringly around the corner of the barn. Spot took three or four tentative steps and paused, wagging his tail. Very slowly (never speak loud or move fast around an animal) the boy bent and found a good-sized stone. He straightened casually, brought his arm back, and threw with all his might. The rock caught Spot squarely in the ribs. He yiped, tucked his tail, and scuttled around the barn, and Bruce chased him, throwing clods and stones and gravel, yelling, "Get out! Go on, get out of here or I'll kick you apart. Get out! Go on!"

So all that spring, while the world dried in the sun and the willows emerged from the floodwater and the mud left by the freshet hardened and caked among their roots, and the grass of the meadow greened and the river brush grew misty with tiny leaves and the dandelions spread yellow among the flats, Bruce tended his colt. While the other boys roamed the bench hills with .22's looking for gophers or rabbits or sage hens, he anxiously superintended the colt's nursing and watched it learn to nibble the grass. While his gang built a darkly secret hide-out in the deep brush beyond Hazard's, he was currying and brushing and trimming the chestnut mane. When packs of boys ran hare and hounds through the town and around the river's slow bends, he perched on the front porch with his slingshot and a can full of small round stones, waiting for stray dogs to appear. He waged a holy war on the dogs until they learned to detour widely around his house, and he never did completely forgive his own dog, Spot. His whole life was wrapped up in the hobbled, leg-ironed chestnut colt with the slow-motion lunging walk and the affectionate nibbling lips.

Every week or so Enich, who was now working out of town at the Half Diamond Bar, rode in and stopped. Always, with that expressionless quiet that was terrible to the boy, he stood and looked the colt over, bent to feel pastern and fetlock, stood back to watch the plunging walk when the boy held out a handful of grass. His expression said nothing; whatever he thought was hidden back of his leathery face as the dark mole was hidden in the crease beside his mouth. Bruce found himself watching that mole sometimes, as if revelation might lie there. But when he pressed Enich to tell him, when he said, "He's getting better, isn't he? He walks better, doesn't he, Mr. Enich? His ankles don't bend so much, do they?" the wrangler gave him little encouragement.

"Let him be a while. He's growin', sure enough. Maybe give him another month."

May passed. The river was slow and clear again, and some of the boys were already swimming. School was almost over. And still Bruce paid attention to nothing but Socks. He willed so strongly that the colt should get well that he grew furious even at Daisy when she sometimes wouldn't let the colt suck as much as he wanted. He took a butcher knife and cut the long tender grass in the fence corners, where Socks could not reach, and fed it to his pet by the handful. He trained him to nuzzle for sugar-lumps in his pockets. And back in his mind was a fear: in the middle of June they would be going out to the homestead again, and if Socks weren't well by that time he might not be able to go.

"Pa," he said, a week before they planned to leave. "How much of a load are we going to have, going out to the homestead?"

"I don't know, wagonful, I suppose. Why?"

"I just wondered." He ran his fingers in a walking motion along the round edge of the dining table, and strayed into the other room. If they had a wagon load, then there was no way Socks could be loaded in and taken along. And he couldn't walk fifty kilometres. He'd get left behind before they got up on the bench, hobbling along like the little crippled boy in the Pied Piper, and they'd look back and see him trying to run, trying to keep up.

That picture was so painful that he cried over it in bed that night. But in the morning he dared to ask his father if they couldn't take Socks along to the farm. His father turned to him eyes as sober as Jim Enich's, and when he spoke it was with a kind of tired impatience. "How can he go? He couldn't walk it."

"But I want him to go, Pa!"

"Brucie," his mother said, "don't get your hopes up. You know we'd do it if we could, if it was possible."

"But Ma..."

His father said, "What you want us to do, haul a broken-legged colt fifty kilometres?"

"He'd be well by the end of the summer, and he could walk back."

"Look," his father said. "Why can't you make up your mind to it? He isn't getting well. He isn't going to get well."

"He is too getting well!" Bruce shouted. He half stood up at the table, and his father looked at his mother and shrugged.

"Please, Bo," she said.

"Well, he's got to make up his mind to it sometime," he said.

Jim Enich's wagon pulled up on Saturday morning, and Bruce was out the door before his father could rise from his chair. "Hi, Mr. Enich," he said.

"Hello, Bub. How's your pony?"

"He's fine," Bruce said. "I think he's got a lot better since you saw him last."

"Uh-huh." Enich wrapped the lines around the whipstock and climbed down. "Tell me you're leaving next week."

"Yes," Bruce said. "Socks is in the back."

When they got into the back yard Bruce's father was there with his hands behind his back, studying the colt as it hobbled around. He looked at Enich. "What do you think?" he said. "The kid here thinks his colt can walk out to the homestead."

"Uh-huh," Enich said. "Well, I wouldn't say that." He inspected the chestnut, scratched between his ears. Socks bobbed, and snuffled at his pockets. "Kid's made quite a pet of him."

Bruce's father grunted. "That's just the trouble."

"I didn't think he could walk out," Bruce said. "I thought we could take him in the wagon, and then he'd be well enough to walk back in in the fall."

"Uh," Enich said. "Let's take his braces off for a minute."

He unbuckled the triple straps on each leg, pulled the braces off, and stood back. The colt stood almost as flat on his fetlocks as he had the morning he was born. Even Bruce, watching with his whole mind tight and apprehensive, could see that. Enich shook his head.

"You see, Bruce?" his father said. "It's too bad, but he isn't getting better. You'll have to make up your mind...."

"He will get better though!" Bruce said. "It just takes a long time, is all." He looked at his father's face, at Enich's, and neither one had any hope in it. But when Bruce opened his mouth to say something else his father's eyebrows drew down in sudden, unaccountable anger, and his hand made an impatient sawing motion in the air.

"We shouldn't have tried this in the first place," he said. "It just tangles everything up." He patted his coat pockets, felt in his vest. "Run in and get me a couple cigars."

Bruce hesitated, his eyes on Enich. "Run!" his father said harshly.

Reluctantly he released the colt's halter rope and started for the house. At the door he looked back, and his father and Enich were talking together, so low that their words didn't carry to where he stood. He saw his father shake his head, and Enich bend to pluck a grass stem. They were both against him, they both were sure Socks would never get well. Well, he would! There was some way.

He found the cigars, came out, watched them both light up. Disappointment was a sickness in him, and mixed with the disappointment was a question. When he could stand their silence no more he burst out with it. "But what are we going to *do*? He's got to have some place to stay."

"Look, kiddo," His father sat down on a sawhorse and took him by the arm. His face was serious and his voice gentle. "We can't take him out there. He isn't well enough to walk, and we can't haul him. So Jim here has offered to buy him. He'll give you three dollars for him, and when you come back, if you want, you might be able to buy him back. That is if he's well. It'll be better to leave him with Jim."

"Well..." Bruce studied the mole on Enich's cheek. "Can you get him better by fall, Mr. Enich?"

"I wouldn't expect it," Enich said. "He ain't got much of a show."

"If anybody can get him better, Jim can," his father said. "How's that deal sound to you?"

"Maybe when I come back he'll be all off his braces and running around like a house afire," Bruce said. "Maybe next time I see him I can ride him." The mole disappeared as Enich tongued his cigar.

"Well, all right then," Bruce said, bothered by their stony-eyed silence. "But I sure hate to leave you behind, Socks, old boy."

"It's the best way all around," his father said. He talked fast, as if he were in a hurry. "Can you take him along now?"

"Oh, gee!" Bruce said. "Today?"

"Come on," his father said. "Let's get it over with."

Bruce stood by while they trussed the colt and hoisted him into the wagon box, and when Jim climbed in he cried out, "Hey, we forgot to put his hobbles back on." Jim and his father looked at each other. His father shrugged. "All right," he said, and started putting the braces back on the trussed front legs. "He might hurt himself if they weren't on," Bruce said. He leaned over the endgate stroking the white blazed face, and as the wagon pulled away he stood with tears in his eyes and the three dollars in his hand, watching the terrified straining of the colt's neck, the bony head raised above the endgate and one white eye rolling.

Five days later, in the sun-slanting, dew-wet spring morning, they stood for the last time that summer on the front porch, the loaded wagon against the front fence. The father tossed the key in his hand and kicked the doorjamb. "Well, goodbye, Old Paint," he said. "See you in the fall."

As they went to the wagon Bruce sang loudly,

Goodbye Old Paint, I'm leavin' Cheyenne,
I'm leavin' Cheyenne, I'm goin' to Montana,
Goodbye, Old Paint, I'm leavin' Cheyenne.

"Turn it off," his father said. "You want to wake up the whole town?" He boosted Bruce into the back end, where he squirmed and wiggled his way neck-deep into the luggage. His mother, turning to see how he was settled, laughed at him. "You look like a baby owl in a nest," she said.

His father turned and winked at him. "Open your mouth and I'll drop in a mouse."

It was good to be leaving; the thought of the homestead was exciting. If he could have taken Socks along it would have been perfect, but he had to admit, looking around at the jammed wagon box, that there sure wasn't any room for him. He continued to sing softly as they rocked out into the road and turned east toward MacKenna's house, where they were leaving the keys.

At the low, sloughlike spot that had become the town's dumpground the road split, leaving the dump like an island in the middle. The boy sniffed at the old familiar smells of rust and tar-paper and ashes and refuse. He had collected a lot of old iron and tea lead and bottles and broken machinery and clocks, and once a perfectly good amberheaded cane, in that old dumpground. His father turned up the right fork, and as they passed the central part of the dump the wind, coming in from the northeast brought a rotten, unbearable stench across them.

"Pee-you!" his mother said, and held her nose. Bruce echoed her. "Pee-you! Pee-you-willy!" He clamped his nose shut and pretended to fall dead.

"Guess I better get to windward of that coming back," said his father.

They woke MacKenna up and left the key and started back. The things they passed were very sharp and clear to the boy. He was seeing them for the last time all summer. He noticed things he had never noticed so clearly before: how the hills came down into the river from the north like three folds in a blanket, how the stovepipe on the shack east of town had a little conical hat on it. He chanted at the things he saw. "Goodbye, old shack. Goodbye, old Frenchman River. Goodbye old Dumpground, goodbye."

"Hold your noses," his father said. He eased the wagon into

the other fork around the dump. "Somebody sure dumped something rotten."

He stared ahead, bending a little, and Bruce heard him swear. He slapped the reins on the team until they trotted. "What?" the mother said. Bruce, half rising to see what caused the speed, saw her lips go flat over her teeth, and a look on her face like the woman he had seen in the traveling dentist's chair, when the dentist dug a living nerve out of her tooth and then got down on his knees to hunt for it, and she sat there half raised in her seat, her face lifted.

"For gosh sakes," he said. And then he saw.

He screamed at them. "Ma, it's Socks! Stop, Pa! It's Socks!"

His father drove grimly ahead, not turning, not speaking, and his mother shook her head without looking around. He screamed again, but neither of them turned. And when he dug down into the load, burrowing in and shaking with long smothered sobs, they still said nothing.

So they left town, and as they wound up the dugway to the south bench there was not a word among them except his father's low, "I thought he was going to take it out of town." None of them looked back at the view they had always admired, the flat river bottom green with spring, its village snuggled in the loops of river. Bruce's eyes, pressed against the coats and blankets under him until his sight was a red haze, could still see through it the bloated, skinned body of the colt, the chestnut hair left a little way above the hooves, the iron braces still on the broken front legs.

Life can be unfair, and people can be cruel. But regardless of the obstacles you face, you can hold on to your pride. Pride in what you can do—pride in where you come from —and pride in who you are.

"IT CAN'T BE HELPED"

Barry Broadfoot

When Japan bombed Pearl Harbor, Hawaii, near the end of World War II, it suddenly seemed like the fighting was at Canada's back door. As a result, the Canadian Government decided that citizens of Japanese origin living on the West Coast were a threat to national security and declared them "enemy aliens." More than 22 000 Japanese-Canadians were stripped of their rights, uprooted from their homes, and forced to live in intern-ment camps. Barry Broadfoot recorded the memories of many of the camp survivors. This is one man's story.

Shikata-ga-nai. That is a Japa-nese phrase. You say it fast. *Shi-kata-ga-nai.* It means "it can't be helped." That's why we did it. *Shi-kata-ga-nai.*

That's why most of us didn't put up a fuss. It is part of our upbringing. When something happens, and it is what we pretty well expect and there is nothing we can do about it, we say *Shikata-*

ga-nai. Everybody knows what it means. Things are beyond our control. We couldn't fight the English from taking my father's fish boat and sending him away to Lucerne. They told my mother she couldn't be a dressmaker anymore. They put us in the camp. It was a long, long train ride and there was mother and four of us kids. I don't know where my oldest brother had gone. Then. He just ran and hid. We got to Sandon and we were tired, oh so tired, and all we had was clothes, some bedclothes, pots, a box of patterns, and my mother's sewing machine. I couldn't even have my air rifle. They had taken it away, too.

My mother was crying when she got off the train. Such a little poky place and the mountains everywhere and I think it was raining. There were Japanese people there and when they heard there was a train of Japanese coming they came down. To help, see that they got in the right houses, where to go. You know, how to do. They said nice things.

My mother was crying and one man came up to her and said, "*Shikata-ga-nai*," and I remember my mother nodding her head and smiling a bit. It can't be helped. Well, it could be helped by me. I was fourteen and I was a tough little bird and I said to this man to

hell with his *shikata-ga-nai*. You know, whether you know it or not, Japanese boys did not use words like that then. Never. Oh yes, in the back alley, with other boys— but never at home, never in front of the older people. Never. It just wasn't done. I had insulted my mother, the friend, everybody in that station.

I remember it well, the humiliation. He took one step toward me and he said, "You are contumacious," and then he hit me one alongside my head and that knocked me spinning. That man was educated. That's some word.

I had to go and apologize to

him next day but I still didn't know what the word meant. But I never forgot it. No, I never forgot it. It was years later before I found a dictionary with it in, the ones at school were no good, and it meant "perverse, wilful." I'm not even sure I expected to find it in the dictionary. I think I even felt it was a high Japanese word I had never heard, but no, it was English all right.

Contumacious. I know that word now.

All I was was a fourteen-year-old kid who didn't know what was happening to me, losing all my friends, going out to this joint in the mountains, just trees and rocks and old buildings around, and I had enough sense to know that if this was *shikata-ga-nai*, then there was something wrong with all of us. I knew it then, fourteen years old, and I know it now.

It could have been helped. We were not cattle. We were human beings, Canadians, and I still say to hell with their *shikata-ga-nai*. I do, although you talk to a lot of Japanese and they still say it. You see, to them it is fate. They had no control over the forces that control them. Fate. It can't be helped. Well, I just didn't happen to believe that, young as I was.

PANACHE

W . P . Kinsella

M e and Frank Fence-post and a few other guys been taking a course the government offer on how to be mechanics. The first year of the course was just about over and Mr. Nichols, our English instructor and counselor was helping some of us write job application letters so we maybe work and earn some money in the summer.

I have to write Frank Fence-post's letters because he is only able to write most of his name.

"Hey, Silas," Frank he say to me, "if we get these letters wrote up all spelled right and all, wouldn't it be better if we could keep them from knowing we is Indians?"

"How we gonna do that?" says Tom Pony. "With names like Silas Ermineskin, Donald Bobtail and Rufus Firstrider, it not going to be so hard for them to guess."

Frank, he finally decide to sign his letters J. Frank Fencepost, so it sound important just like the Mayor of Wetaskiwin, who is Mr. J. William Oberholtzer. We all laugh a lot about that, but Mr. Nichols he say that us guys will maybe get to work in a mill somewhere but they put Frank in Public Relations, whatever that is.

The last talk that Mr. Nichols gave us in English class is one that I never forget. It is Mr. Nichols who get me to write down stories and he say if I keep on maybe someday I write some good enough to get printed.

His lecture was all about a French word called "panache," which he say is, and I write it down real careful: *the ability to exude the effect of a plume on a helmet*.

He show us pictures of knights with big curled feathers above their armour, and he tell us that anybody can act like he got them feathers. If we stand tall and have the right attitude then we can have panache and look like we warriors wearing a war bonnet and holding a lance, even if we really just got on jeans and a T-shirt. Then we look at pictures of Indian chiefs and Mr. Nichols say that they got more nobility and panache than knights ever had. I make sure I remember what it is he tells us but I don't figure I have a chance to use it for maybe a long time.

Me and Frank and Tom Pony all got hired by a coal mine out near Jasper, Alberta, and a good long way from our reserve here at Hobbema. The mine is at a place called Luscar, what used to be a town but ain't anymore, and the mine ain't underground like you would suppose but is up top and called a strip mine. The mine is called Cardinal Coal Mines and Frank he figures that it must be owned by Indians. We got about twenty families named Cardinal on the reserve and we guess maybe one of them run it.

The nearest town is called Hinton, and the three of us take the bus up there and get us a basement room and board with a white lady who says we should call her Gran. Her husband runs the movie machine at the picture show and he say he let us guys in free to all the movies.

"That's really white of you," Frank says. I kick his ankle and when we alone I tell him not to make fun of these people 'cause they is really trying to be nice on us. None of us ever been in a white people's house before—they even got three goldfish in a big glass jar.

Gran, she serves us more food than I ever seen before, and she say she gonna have to fatten us up, especially Tom Pony who is little and got hollow cheeks. She say he looks like he never had a good meal in his life.

Boy, this is sure nice people, and things look good for us until the first day we start work.

We have to take a company bus about forty kilometres out to the mine and boy do the guys we gonna work with ever look funny at us on the way out.

"Maybe they don't have no Indians in this part of the country," whispers Frank.

"Maybe they do," say Tom Pony.

I never even dream there are places like this mine. They got there what they call trucks but they is three men tall and the cab sits off to one side like they missed when they put it together. I am almost two metres tall but I don't even come to the top of one wheel. These trucks go up and down narrow little trails and then back up to the very edge of what sure look like hell to me, and dump their load. The rocks go down, what the foreman say is over a hundred fifty metres into a pit that he says been burning for maybe twenty years. There is smoke hang around over everything, make it like it cloudy all the time.

We don't have to drive the trucks and I sure glad about that. We just gonna do odd jobs. That is if we ever get to work, 'cause when the shifts change everybody have a big meeting with the foreman. We don't have to figure too hard to guess that it about us.

All the men wear bright red coveralls and yellow hardhats and what with the dust and smoke hang around all over, it sure remind me of a picture I seen once of all the devils in hell.

"We ain't gonna have no so-and-so Indians work here," says a big man with a beer belly and yellow hair.

"I don't like it no better than you, Gunderson," say the foreman. Then he goes into a long story about how the government gives money to the mine, but if the mine takes the money it got to hire some guys like us.

They argue for a long time. Gunderson say there no way the men gonna work if we work.

"Look," say the foreman, "I'm gonna put the tall one up in the tower with a pencil and the other two on odd jobs. You won't even know they're here."

Gunderson went and had a pow-wow with the other men.

"As long as they don't touch none of the equipment. We don't want them to screw nothing up. It's dangerous enough here without guys like that working on our machines." I can tell right then that we ain't gonna get to do no mechanic work even though that's what we been trained to do for the last year.

What happens is we don't get to do much of anything. I count the loads each truck dumps but some other guy counts them too. Frank sweep the floor of the garage and when he finish he sweep it again. Tom Pony stand out near where the trucks back up. He is supposed to wave them back and signal them when to stop which would be an important job except that all the drivers they been working here a long time and they put the truck where they want it and don't pay no attention to Tom except for a couple of them I think tried to run him over once or twice.

"They'll get used to you in a few days," said Gran, while she was packing us the biggest lunches I ever seen with sandwiches made with real ham and fresh tomatoes. We only been here a couple of weeks and already Tom Pony look like he is put on weight.

"You just seem a little strange to them," Gran went on. "Once they get to know you everything will be okay." Gran, she remind me of my Ma who is always believe everything gonna be okay too, no matter how bad it get.

"They is plenty strange to us too," says Frank, "Don't nobody ever think of that?"

Gunderson, he have all the men except us sign their names on a paper sheet that he gonna send to the head office of the mine, so they have to get rid of us.

But the paper it never got sent because that afternoon Gunderson have his accident. I was way up in the tower so all I could do was watch. Gunderson is back his truck up to the edge of the pit but he come up real fast try to scare Tom Pony and go a metre too far and the rock start to crumble away from under the back wheels. He tries to pull forward but all that keeps the truck from going down is the forward pull of the wheels.

"Jump!" yells the foreman, but Gunderson is all tangled up and hangs there like a monkey on a stick I seen once at the Royal American Shows at the Ponoka Stampede. Some say that Gunderson got his overalls caught on the gearshift or that he had his boot jammed under the brake. It depend who you listen to tells the story, but he is sure one long time getting out of that cab.

What happens next I don't believe if I don't see. Tom Pony been waving him back and he is right at the edge looking at where the rock breaking away. Afterward, everybody say how Tom is a hero and all, and what a good Indian he is because he save Gunderson's life even though he trying to get Tom fired. I don't think Tom even knew who was in the cab. But I put myself in his place and figure that if that truck go over, guess who gonna get blamed, the Indian or the driver? I figure Tom was more trying to save our jobs than anything else, but I never tell anybody else that. It funny how people, even big tough ones like Gunderson and his friends, like to believe in heroes.

Tom Pony he get right out on the edge of the pit dig in his foot and push against the wheel of the truck. I only heard about someone show strength like he did then.

On the reserve they tell about one time Moses Louis rolled his Volkswagen on top of himself and Mrs. Louis she picked it up off him 'cause she was the only one around and if she didn't he'd of died.

"Jump!" the foreman keeps yelling and someone is climb up and pull on Gunderson's one leg that hangs out the door, but no one goes back to help Tom Pony. He just pushes against the back wheel and from way up where I am I can tell that for a few seconds that truck stops crawling backward. Those few seconds give Gunderson enough time to untangle and finally he is jump clear. Tom Pony ain't so lucky. He got no place to jump clear to and the rig goes over the bank and takes Tom with it.

That night we is all sit around the bar down to the Timberline Hotel in Hinton. Gunderson is our best friend now and so is just about everybody else. They sure buy us a lot of beer and say what good guys we are. Gunderson say that there should be a memorial of some kind for Tom Pony, even if they never gonna be able to get his body up out of the burning pit. He pass the hat around the bar and collect a whole lot of bills, mostly tens and twenties.

"We're going to buy a stone and put it on the side of the hill by the mine entrance for everybody to see," Gunderson say. Everybody is some happy.

"Hey, Partner," Frank say to me, "you figure they figure if they buy us enough beer it gonna bring Tom Pony back to life?"

Me and Frank went with Gunderson the next morning down to the tombstone place. Gunderson talked to a man in a suit and a bright red tie who pointed out the different stones in the yard.

"This here's the best we can get for the money we got,"

Gunderson says finally, point at a shiny black stone with what looked like little flecks of gold in it.

"It's okay with me," I say. It be better if we give the money to Tom Pony's mother, but I don't say that.

"What do you want on it?" say the man in the suit.

"Why couldn't we just take the stone back with us to Hobbema?" say Frank. "We could take it on the bus. I buy it a ticket myself and it can sit beside me just like Tom Pony did on the way down."

I was trying to think of what to put on the stone.

"His name?" said the man.

"Tom Pony."

"Thomas…"

"No. Just Tom."

"Date of birth?"

Frank and me looked at each other. "He was eighteen," I said.

"You want an inscription? You get up to six words free."

I couldn't think of anything for a while, then I remember Mr. Nichols' last lecture to us.

"Panache," I say.

"What's that?" said the tombstone man, who was making notes with a pencil in a scribbler.

"It's what I want on Tom Pony's tombstone. Panache."

I had to spell it for him about six times before he got it right.

"What is it anyway, some kind of Indian word?"

"Yeah, I think it is," I say.

THE BLUEBERRY PICKERS

Sigrun Goodman Zatorsky

1932 was a black year for Annie Koblanchuk. It was a black year for many people in Winnipeg. The economy was in depression and for most, unemployment, soup kitchens and being on relief were more the normal condition than the exception. These things Annie could endure. But on his first day at a job which finally showed promise of steady employment, Mike Koblanchuk was killed by a steam locomotive in the Canadian Pacific Railyards. He left to his wife, Annie, a legacy consisting of two weeks prepaid rent, fifty dollars in quarters in the tobacco tin in the dresser drawer and three young children to be provided for. She used the fifty dollars to bury Mike. When the two-week rental period was all but spent and promises of assistance from church and welfare agency still remained only promises, Annie was compelled to put aside her grieving and face the future. She must exchange a portion of her role as homemaker, the only occupation she had ever known, for that of wage-earner.

All evening while she scrubbed the sixth floor offices and lavatory, Annie had been remembering how Mike had enjoyed taking her and the kids on outings, inexpensive outings to be sure; picnics in Assiniboine Park, berry picking and hazelnut gathering out by the cement works and walking, just plain walking—anywhere, anytime. Oi! That Mike could walk! Lengthy strides that stretched his long sinewy legs and brought his big size twelve shoes down hard on the heel, the exertion swelling his chest and manufacturing muscle on shoulders already made muscular through hard labour.

She swished her grimy floor rag across cold white tile, smiling as she remembered the children endeavouring to make their short legs keep pace with Mike's long ones. Five-year-old Nicky, whose knees were invariably imbedded with either particles from the old cinder sidewalks or slivers from the wooden ones, had to hold Mike's hand. But young Johnny, who was then eight and practically grown, strode manfully by his father's side, half walking, half running, to keep up. Annie and the youngest child, Orysia, were usually far behind. Ah, those were the good times.

Bozha! Bozha! Why was he taken? Nine years we are in Canada and all the time he works so hard, so many jobs, waiting for the steady job, then? Annie's eyes filled, blurring her vision, and she wiped away the moisture with the sleeve of her sweater—Mike's old sweater.

Almost a year after his death, Annie found that her tears differed from the bitter, despairing flood she had wept at first. She was resigned now to the fact that he was gone, that she was father, mother and provider to his children; but these occasional tears were therapeutic, slowly soothing and healing a deep wound.

Annie sighed and stood up, wiping her hands on her apron. She blew her nose on bathroom tissue, sighed, and went back to the work at hand. Renewing her wash water, she eased her bulk in under the sink, carefully, for this angular projection and Annie's head usually came in contact with one another at least once during each evening.

When she had cleaned the fifth and fourth floors, Annie, with aching back and stiff legs (for she always scrubbed on her hands and knees rather than stand with a mop as Mrs. Ryan did), met her co-worker on the third floor, where the two women sat down in one of the offices to rest and talk.

"Well, Mrs. Koblanchuk," Mrs. Ryan sighed as she sank into a leather-upholstered chair. "Don't get no easier, does it?"

She swung her feet up onto the glass-topped desk, and reaching into her pocket, the only part of her sweater that had not begun to unravel, brought forth the butt of a cigarette and lit it ostentatiously with an ornate lighter from the desk top. Annie gasped slightly at her partner's daring, for a feeling of servility prevented her from reclining in an executive chair and she humbly chose instead a straight-backed chair at the side of the desk.

"Not so bad." Annie shrugged her shoulders and smiled at Mrs. Ryan, then watched with fascination as the other woman smoked. Annie could not condone the cigarette habit, but, where Mrs. Ryan was concerned, neither could she peremptorily condemn it—and certainly not aloud—for though Mrs. Ryan admitted that smoking was a vice, Annie knew that it was also her third floor reward.

Annie's cleaning partner presented a comical spectacle on scrubbing evenings, with skirts tucked into the bottom of her girdle, making it appear that she wore baggy bloomers; thin, bony legs autographed liberally with knotted varicose veins, and old shapeless shoes that seemed grotesquely huge and out of proportion to her legs. Still, Annie was forced to admit that where her char-partner appeared ludicrous due to her gauntness, she, Annie, must look contrarily humorous, for her inexpensive but sometimes starchy diet (she seldom made soup without also making tystau, the little pieces of dough, to go with it), had forced her figure beyond her original 'pleasingly plump' stage. Where Mrs. Ryan appeared to have the same meager dimensions from top to bottom; Annie was full-bossomed, thick-waisted and perhaps too amply cushioned in the posterior region. But she wasted no precious time fretting about her figure. She lived only for her children.

Mrs. Ryan inhaled deeply on her cigarette, then spoke, releasing small puffs of smoke with each word. This performance always held Annie's attention, for she half expected that when smoke could be expelled alternately from Mrs. Ryan's nose and mouth, it might also come from her ears.

"Where'r ye going' for yer holiday, Mrs. Koblanchuk? Just stayin' to home, I guess."

"No..." Annie brightened suddenly. "I take my kids out to fresh air. I take them..." she paused, "blueberry picking!"

She announced the proposed event as though it had been in preparation for some time. In fact, it had just come to mind. Annie's tendency to precipitate action was evident in her hastily conceived idea for the holiday, but she had been moved by the evening's melancholy and the conviction that she must take her husband's place in the lives of her children.

"But where would yez go? Ye have to go a long ways fer blueberries, ye know. They ain't growin' on Portage and Main."

Although the two women considered themselves to be good friends, each seemed to possess the knack, probably unintentional, of antagonizing the other.

"I go out where Mike and me always go. Always lots berries." Annie used her hands for emphasis.

"Humph!" said Mrs. Ryan, "and how ye going' to get to this here place?" She closed one eye against the curl of cigarette smoke and looked at Annie out of the other. "Would ye like to borry me chauffeur fer the day?"

She slapped her knee and laughed heartily at her own joke. Mrs. Ryan was well aware of the hardships Annie encountered in her endeavours to support her family, and Annie, she recalled with some chagrin, had been aghast at her suggestion that she might have a little more money to feed the children if she did as so many were doing and sold a little homemade wine.

"I feed my kids!" Annie had responded indignantly. "I make soup, perohi, holopchy, kasha. I make everything! I don't need bootleg!"

Annie continued her defence of the picking district. "I know a place. We get ride with farmer. Lots nice farmer. So..."

She turned up the palms of her hands and shrugged her shoulders as though to finalize the subject. Now the old lady had settled it, she with her doubting attitude. Annie would go picking come hell or high water and ironically, before the holiday ended she would experience a little of the former and an unexpected amount of the latter.

The following Sunday morning found Annie and the three Koblanchuk children, boys in their good tweed caps (which were to be removed when they reached the bush) and Orysia with her long hair freshly plaited, trudging through the bush, and events had transpired much as she had predicted. They had ridden the streetcar to the end of the line, then managed a ride on the first farm truck that had come along.

The August day showed promise of being hot and muggy. When the truck driver had reluctantly deposited Annie and her brood at a spot on the highway which she thought familiar, he had warned of the possibility of an oncoming storm. But the enthusiasm of the blueberry pickers was not to be dampened on this beautiful day.

Patches of blueberry plants were soon located in various spots among the bushes and rocks, for the district had, as prophesied by Annie, 'lots blueberries.' The children darted happily about picking and eating the whitish-blue fruit and enjoying themselves to the fullest. This was the way she had hoped it would be. She spoke so incessantly of Mike as they roamed through the bush that it was as though 'Tatu' were with them; making jokes, teasing, encouraging their efforts. She told them proudly how their father had taught himself to speak and read English (Annie as a homemaker, had remained close to her ethnic neighbourhood and learned more slowly) how he had once made this profound statement or carried out that clever action, and if Mike Koblanchuk had been less than a saint, his children would be none the wiser. He lived in them, and Annie was perpetuating his memory with every word.

Exuberant happiness swelled her heart and brought tears to her eyes as she watched the laughing faces of her children, and the joy and simulated sunshine that was radiated from the little group as they pushed deeper into the bush hid the black clouds that had been gathering unheeded overhead.

The rain came suddenly, in torrents, as Annie and the children had barely finished a late lunch. The deluge sent them scurrying to the shelter of a tall tree.

"We can't stay here, Ma!" Johnny shouted above the rain. "If there's lightning, it'll take the easiest route to the ground to where we are!"

Annie was skeptical, for she had always believed that a tree offered the best shelter during a storm, but she gathered the younger children and followed the boy to where he had pointed out a precipice of rock and fallen trees. They scrambled up the high, flat rock, wet, breathless and minus the largest pail of berries which Annie had kicked over in her hasty flight. The new shelter was ideal, for dead pines and other branches had fallen across the top of a jutting rock, forming a protective roof at an angle over their heads. The children still held their little pails of berries and Annie had managed to scoop up her old shopping bag, with her handbag, blanket and the children's sweaters. Now they sat huddled together to wait out the rain.

Inwardly, Annie derided herself for not having foreseen the rainstorm. After all, the farmer had warned her. To the children, however, she spoke cheerfully and joked about weaving a basket to float them home like Moses in the bullrushes. Had she known of the torrents of water still to be poured down on them from the darkened heavens, she would have bitten her tongue; had she been able to foretell that she would sit on this rock for almost three days within walking distance of semi-dry land, she would have been inconsolable.

When late in the afternoon the rainfall had not ceased, Annie began to grow uneasy, the children restless. The dark clouds had not dissipated and the water stood several centimetres deep in the small gullies and crevices below their shelter. Nightfall would soon bring total blackness, making it impossible to find the trail back to the highway. Even now Annie was uncertain in which direction the highway lay, for their quest for berries had taken them on many twists and turns through the bush. If the sun would show even a faint glow through the clouds, she would ascertain east and west, and she knew that the road lay to the west.

She was about to set out alone to reconnoiter, then decided this would be foolhardy. Leaving her children alone with darkness rapidly closing in, losing her own way in the bush, would place them in worse straits than before. She weighed the situation a moment longer, then made her decision. They would stay the night! With the rising of the sun and the cessation of the rain, they could be well on their way in the early morning. They had had a meal this day and the children had their little pails of berries. There were sweaters and a blanket and they had secured the most salient requirement: shelter. Annie prepared them for sleep—she and Johnny with their backs against the rock and the younger children on their laps—secure in the knowledge that she had made the correct decision.

She dozed fitfully throughout the night and when at times she awakened, the rain was still falling, though she could not estimate in the country blackness to what extent or measure.

With the first grey light of dawn, Annie awoke with a start and looked about her. Her pulse quickened and she blinked her eyes in disbelief. Water covered everything around them! The small, water-filled gullies of yesterday had merged to form a huge lake which completely surrounded the rock upon which she and the children sat. They were marooned on a stony island in the middle of the bush! Annie was seized with panic. She rushed to the edge of the rock.

"Oi! What happened?" she cried aloud. Running to the other side, the idiom was repeated. "Oi!"

Suddenly Johnny was beside her.

"Gee, Ma. What are we going to do?"

Orysia, who had been thrown unceremoniously from Annie's knee, ran wailing to her mother and Annie, hobbled by the child clinging to her leg, limped back and forth, hand to her cheek, dragging Orysia with her.

When Annie had partially regained her composure and had quieted the children, she sat down on the blanket and began to remove her shoes and stockings. Bidding her children to sit quietly, she waded into the direction of the tall tree under which they had first taken shelter. She had chosen this goal at random, the tree being the only familiar landmark visible. Halfway to her destination, she sank into water to her waist. Suddenly, uneven footing on the slippery rocks threw her off balance and she found herself sputtering and thrashing about in the murky water. With great exertion she righted herself and turned back toward the shelter. The uncertainty of her foothold forced her to make her way by grasping protruding branches for support, and more than once she wavered like a novice on ice skates. Back once more on the rock, Annie sank down heavily; a picture of sodden despair. But no, she thought, as she caught a glimpse of the children's faces, she must not look too pitiable. Nicky was snickering behind his hand and Orysia's crying had turned to giggling. Even sober-faced Johnny smiled sheepishly when nudged by his brother.

"You sure looked funny, Ma," Nicky managed between staccato titters. "You're all covered with mud and you got branches in your hair like a reindeer."

At sight of his mother's stern look, he hurriedly covered his mouth with his hand.

"So? Funny, eh?" She shook her finger at him. "I don't do funny tricks in the water, I'm drown! See..." She pointed to her wet clothes.

At his mother's last outburst, Nicky could no longer contain his mirth. "You're not drowned, Ma!" he guffawed. "You're right here talking to us."

The three children laughed together now and Annie could not maintain her anger. There was an infectiousness in the laughter of her children that Annie had never been able to resist. A small branch dangled across her face and the humour of the incident suddenly struck her. She began to chuckle. So? She was wet. She would dry out. She would not shrink, unfortunately. They were all alive and together. Someone would soon come to look for them.

"Well, Ma?" Johhny enquired later when Annie had replaced her stockings and shoes. "What do we do now?"

"We wait," she replied matter-of-factly. "Soon someone comes."

Johnny looked at her seriously. "Who, Ma? Who knows we're here?"

"Maybe Mrs. Krawchuk..." Annie began. Mrs. Krawchuk was the downstairs neighbour who looked in on the children evenings while Annie worked.

"Don't you remember, Ma? She's gone to see her daughter while you're on holidays. What about Mrs. Ryan?"

Annie shook her head. No, Mrs. Ryan would be doing Annie's scrubbing according to a reciprocal agreement, grumbling about her extra workload and envying Annie her vacation. Oh! What of the farmer? Annie's hopes died as quickly as they had come to life. No, the farmer had no way of knowing that they had not already gone home; his interest had ended at the highway. They would probably not be missed for at least a week!

Entertaining the faint hope that someone might be in the vicinity, Annie stood at the edge of the rock and began shouting for help. She exhorted the children to imitate her performance, and soon the entire family circled the periphery of the island, shouting a chorus of 'halloo's' like a team of mountain climbers testing the peaks for ice falls. Nicky, carried away by his enthusiasm, began to yodel, until a sharp rap on the head brought a halt to his Alpine-like endeavour. There was no response to their cries.

Annie put one of the small pails out to catch the rain for drinking water; there were too many little crawly things, too much mud in the water that stood around them. The children ate the berries that remained in their pails and a rummage through Annie's handbag brought forth a contribution to the bill of fare—a dilapidated package of last winter's cough drops. These she distributed, stating that they were more sugar than medication anyway, and something sweet could help sustain them for awhile. There was no other food that day.

Through a second night Annie held her children close— cold, hungry, the two youngest whimpering—and prayed that the rain might cease. She was sure that God had become familiar with His friend, Annie Koblanchuk, during this last troubled year, for she had spoken to Him often.

The following morning, Annie was assured that the good Lord had not grown tired of her constant petitions, for upon opening her eyes she discovered to her joy that the rain had indeed stopped.

With a sigh of relief, she reached down to shake the children but touched instead the cold, smooth body of a snake! It was curled up near Nicky's leg. Annie drew back her hand in revulsion. She shivered, not knowing whether the feeling came from the slithery touch of the reptile or the fear of forcing it into action if she dared move again.

"Don't be scared, Ma." It was Johnny's voice. "It's only a big garter snake. They don't hurt you."

He snatched the snake quickly and flung it over the far side of the rock.

"I hope it lands some place dry," he said solemnly. "It was probably here before we were."

Annie looked thoughtfully at her elder son. So many times since Mike's death, this boy had sustained her, had become her benefactor when she hastily undertook projects which she found herself unable to complete. And it was Johnny who had unintentionally broken down the wall of self-pity Annie had built around herself. She had gone one night to investigate sounds emanating from the kitchen where Johnny and his brother slept on a pull-out couch near the coal and wood range. Someone was crying, but trying desperately to stifle his sobs under the feather perrana. She had gently pulled back the corner of the comforter and found Johnny clutching an old photograph of his father. Wiping the tears from the picture with the sleeve of his nightshirt, he avoided Annie's eyes with a display of boyish shame at having been discovered in the act of crying. Annie had realized for the first time that she was not alone in her grief. This child, and in their own way the little ones, felt the loss of their father as deeply as she as an adult felt the loss of her husband. She had taken her boy in her arms then and they had cried together.

"You know what, Johnny?" Annie said brightly. "The rain stops and soon we go."

Johnnie held up the palms of his hands.

"Hey, Ma! You're right! The water's gone down a little!"

The sky remained grey and overcast, but even termination of the rain was heartening.

It was Johnny who discovered the mushrooms growing in the lichen near the rock. The little mound had been concealed from view until he had began checking for hidden nests of snakes. Annie gave each child four mushrooms and herself three.

"I don't want any." Nicky wrinkled up his face.

Annie's gaze was steady. "Eat!" she said.

The boy turned his head away from the proferred food, and instantly Annie grasped his jaw, forcing his mouth open.

"You chew slow," she said, poking a piece of mushroom into his mouth and working his jaws up and down with her hand. "Like this."

He gagged and Annie's face grew red with anger. The child, making a wry face, chewed and swallowed. He knew from experience that he had no alternative. His mother would keep him alive even if she had to half kill him to do it.

The light repast having been consumed, Annie felt cheered and told the children that when they were back home, she would make nalysnyncky with homemade applesauce as a special treat.

By midday, the sun was beginning to peek through the clouds, and its bright, warming rays brought a rejuvenating effect. Annie passed the time waiting for the water to recede by telling the children stories of when she and Mike had come to Canada. She drew gales of laughter with the tale of Mike and other immigrant bushworkers who, never having seen a beaver, were warned by fellow workers to keep a wary lookout for this huge beast. It had not been difficult for the practical jokers to convince the newcomers that the beaver must be an animal of Herculean proportions, for they had seen the felled trees and great dams left in its wake. Being introduced to the little Canadian beaver by his laughing fellow workers proved to be an enlightening and an embarrassing experience for Mike Koblanchuk.

By mid-afternoon, Annie was able to ascertain her proper direction. The muddy water had receded sufficiently to allow egress from the bush, and to the delight of the children, they travelled barefoot, their shoes tied together and strung around their necks, their stockings trussed into the toes of their shoes.

Their course, it was apparent to a breathless and perspiring Annie, was entirely uphill. When, to her consternation, they encountered terrain which held only the remaining traces of rainfall, she paused to look back on the locale which had served as their abode for the past two and one half days. It was a valley! A large section of land with a gradual decline so densely covered with trees and bush that one walked into it without realizing its depth. And when the rain began, she had stationed her children in the centre, oblivious to the fact that the higher ground around them was rejecting the downpour and sending the runoff down upon them.

Annie was again fortunate, upon reaching the highway, to flag down a passing truck and, bouncing along in the back of the vehicle, she thought about how badly her holiday had gone. She had only herself to blame, of course—and possibly the weather for its inconsistency—but as she listened to the excited exchanges between her children, she conceded that, yes, it had been as they were describing it: an adventure, one that had ended well.

The following Monday work night, when the generalities of work vacation had been discussed, Mrs. Ryan, with suggestive glances at Annie's old shopping bag, talked around but never quite mentioned the topic of blueberries.

"Oh," Annie's hand dove into the bag. "I bring you blueberries."

She had not volunteered details of the berry picking expedition, having been punished sufficiently without hearing Mrs. Ryan's 'I told ye so' on every floor.

Mrs. Ryan's face brightened. Her husband was extremely fond of blueberry pie.

"It was nice of ye to think of me at all, Mrs. Koblanchuk. Have ye got enough fer yerselves, then?"

"I think we have enough of blueberries," Annie said with deep sincerity.

Mrs. Ryan took possession of the gift and in a rare show of affection placed her thin hand on Annie's sleeve, squeezing her arm.

"Ye've got a good heart, ye have," she said with an embarrassed sniff. "And I might have known that if Annie Koblanchuk says she's goin' blueberry pickin', she'll do just that!"

Annie proceeded to the closet for her pail and brush with an unusual warmth about her being, not withstanding a slight tinge of guilt. But it was worth it; the satisfaction and joy of giving more than equalled the amount of cabbage soup she and the kids would have to subsist on to pay for the blueberries she had purchased in the North End Market.

*Is there such a thing as fate? If your future is already
decided, would you want to know what's in store for you?
Think carefully before you answer—are you sure you
want to know everything?*

TO CHEAT DEATH

John Anthony Adams

Not being of a superstitious nature, Sgt. Nick Alkemade had no more than the normal fears of flying a wartime mission on his thirteenth raid over Berlin. The British bomber kept its steady course through the moon-brightened sky, dropped its bombs, and turned to fly away from the burning city. But March, 1944 was a very dangerous time to be a crewman in a British bomber. During the previous five months the constantly sharpening German anti-aircraft defences had hammered over one thousand English bombers out of the night skies.

Suddenly the crew members of Alkemade's bomber were made aware of the German fighter on their tail by the crashes of shells from winking cannons directed at them. One shell splintered and blew away the transparent blister covering Alkemade's tail turret, and he found himself staring directly out into space at the black fighter, its cannons still flashing. He fired his tail guns and watched the fighter plunge down into the night with one of its two engines a spurt of flame.

But his bomber was fatally stricken. Burning fuel whipped into the exposed turret as he desperately tried to shield his face with his arm. He heard the pilot's order to bail out and pushed open the tail turret doors to reach for his parachute pack on its rack at the back of the fuselage—kept there because there was no room to wear a parachute while squeezed into the narrow space of the tail turret. Alkemade saw his parachute wreathed in flames, the canopy case already blackening into ash. He realized that he was about to die, and the excruciating pain of the flames made it easy to choose the manner of his death. Better to die from a painless fall than from burning to death! He flung himself backward into space. The fall did not bring terror, but a feeling of great calm.

"I hadn't time to think—things had happened too swiftly. Less than a minute had elapsed since the Junkers 88 (the German nightfigher) set fire to our gas tanks. And now I was falling through space, almost fifty-five hundred metres above Germany.

"I felt a strange peace away from that shriveling heat. As I plunged toward eternity I felt an enjoyment of the cool air rushing over my blistered face. I saw stars between my feet. Falling headfirst I thought casually. If this was dying it was nothing to be afraid of, only a pleasant experience. My only thoughts of an earthly nature were regrets over not saying good-bye to my friends. I was due for leave the following Sunday. It was a shame to miss that. I'd heard that a falling body reaches a hundred ninety-five kilometres per hour. From over five kilometres up, I had ninety seconds to live. One minute and a half to bring to a close a very ordinary life.

"I blacked out. Awareness returned slowly—first as a point of light in a sea of darkness. I tried to think what it was. A star. I was cold, bitterly cold. My arms and legs felt paralyzed. I struggled to sit up. Then it came to me, with an overwhelming shock.

"Oh my God, I'm alive!

"This was no blasphemy, only a heartfelt prayer of thanksgiving. There had been a miracle, but my mind was still too numb to think on it. I ran my hands over my body and limbs, probing. I felt an agonizing pain in my back and shoulders. I was sore and still. My head throbbed. I identified each ache

separately, and marveled that there were not more."

The fire in the bomber had burned Alkemade's face, hands, and legs, but he was in incredibly good shape for having fallen over five kilometres. A moderate concussion, bad scalp cut, strained back, twisted knee, and a deep splinter wound in his thigh were the extent of his injuries from the fall. He pulled matches and cigarettes out of his pocket, lit a match, and saw that he was lying in a snow bank. As he lay back in the snow, shakily puffing a cigarette, he saw the reason for his amazing survival. Above, the moonlight filtered down through the interlaced branches of tall fir trees which had slowed his fall, dropping him onto dense underbrush, which in turn cushioned him still further before his final stop on the snowbank.

Alkemade, his clothes in

shreds and his flying boots lost, tried to stand up on legs that weren't cooperating. The cold was getting to him, and he decided that freezing to death would be worse than trying to get help, even though he would be a prisoner in enemy territory. Blowing the whistles attached to his tunic started some distant shouts, and soon a party of Germans found him, put him on a canvas, and dragged him to a nearby farmhouse. The kindly woman there gave him some strengthening eggnog while they waited for two Gestapo men to arrive. The men took him to a small hospital where doctors cut away his clothes and bathed him, and then to a private room for interrogation.

One of the Gestapo men asked Alkemade what he had done with his parachute. When he replied that he didn't have one—that he had jumped over five kilometres without a chute—the unbelieving German lost his temper, slapped him across the face, and demanded to know where the English tail gunner had buried it. The interrogation continued for days, but the Germans never accepted his story.

After three weeks, Alkemade was taken to Dulag Luft, near Frankfurt, for final interrogation before going to a prisoner of war camp. He repeated his story and was summarily ordered into solitary confinement for a week to encourage him to come up with a more believable version of his arrival in Germany. Finally, in the middle of the night, he realized how to convince his captors he was telling the truth.

The next morning, when he was brought in front of Lt. Hans Feidal, a Luftwaffe officer, Alkemade said he could prove the story of his parachuteless jump if they would bring him the harness he had worn. This was done, and the officer was shown that the hooks and lift webs attached to the clips which should have held the chest canopy pack were still tied down with thread. If the chute had been used the threads would have broken as the lift webs were pulled free. Lieutenant Feidal turned the harness over and over with a look of astonishment as he realized the truth of the Englishman's claim.

Suddenly the German view of Alkemade made a right-angle turn, and from a despised POW he became a figure of awe. The German airmen were a tireless audience, urging him to tell and retell his story, laughing and congratulating him on being alive, and pressing on him rum, cigarettes, and candy. Arriving at the POW camp, Alkemade continued to receive celebrity treatment. Lieutenant Feidal requested the Senior Allied Officer to record for Sergeant Alkemade that his story had been investigated and found true. So Flight Lt. H. J. Moore tore a blank flyleaf from a Bible and wrote as Feidal dictated:

> It has been investigated and corroborated by the German authorities that the claim of Sergeant Alkemade, No. 1431537 RAF, is true in all respects, namely, that he has made a descent from five thousand, five hundred metres without a parachute and made a safe landing without injuries, the parachute having been burnt in the aircraft. He landed in snow among young fir trees.
> Corroboration witnessed by
> Signed:
> F/Lt. H. J. Moore (SBO)
> F/S R. R. Lamb
> F/S T. A. Jones

Feeling "like a freak" in the POW camp and being the talk of the compound was not an all-bad experience, and Sgt. Alkemade was liberated in May, 1945.

Alkemade welcomed the opportunity to return to a safer, duller life after the war, but he was to continue his series of dangerous escapades in peacetime. In 1946, shortly after demobilization, he started working in a chemical factory. One day he had to climb down into a pit to pump out a pool of liquid which was generating poisonous chlorine gas. After about half of the liquid had been removed, Alkemade received a severe electrical shock from the pump and, as the jolt staggered his body, the gas mask fell off his face. He was nearly asphyxiated by the time his fellow workers carried him out of the pit.

A few weeks later at the same factory, Alkemade was siphoning sulfuric acid when the pipe burst, drenching his face and arms with the acid. He might have been fatally burned except for a forty-gallon drum of limewash which was nearby. Alkemade immediately dived headfirst into the drum, neutralized the acid, and escaped with first degree burns. After recovering from the acid spill, Alkemade returned to the deadly factory only to be knocked flat by a three-metre tall piece of steel which broke off and fell on top of him. The men who lifted the steel and pulled Alkemade out feared that he had been killed, but he was only bruised. Still, Alkemade had had enough of the chemical factory. He left to work as a furniture salesman.

THE PREMEDITATED DEATH OF SAMUEL GLOVER

Hugh   Garner

t's been nothing but questions all day at the office. Every few minutes one of the other draftsmen would come over to my board and ask me about Sam's death. "What happened last night? Were you with him? Did it knock him down? Run over him? How'd he look? Was there much blood?"

They have no idea what it's like seeing a friend get killed like that, and having to answer all the questions by the police, the taxi company lawyer, and then by the fellows at work the next day. I'm going to tell it once more, the whole thing, and then I'm through.

Every night at five o'clock for the last seven or eight years Sam Glover and I have taken the elevator together, going home. Sam would buy his evening paper in the lobby, and then we'd walk up the street as far as Queen where we separated, Sam to take a westbound streetcar, and me to take one going east.

It got to be a habit, this three-block walk, and I enjoyed it because Sam was an interesting old fellow to talk to. He was a bachelor who lived with a married sister away out in the west end of town. From some of the things he told me on these short walks I learned that he was a believer in things like fate and premeditation. It was his favourite subject, and sometimes he'd point to people who passed us on the street and say, "There goes a man hurrying to his fate," or "He wants to reach his rendezvous, that one."

When I'd laugh, he'd say, "You'll find out some day that it's no joke. I've seen it happen. Every man is predestined to meet his death at a time and place already chosen, my boy."

I'd laugh and shake my head.

It was about three years ago that Sam told me where he was going to die. We were waiting for the lights to change at the intersection of Adelaide Street, when Sam said, "This is the place where fate is going to catch up to me."

I looked down at him and laughed, thinking he was joking. He was the type of mousy little guy who would joke like that—or dismember a corpse.

"You may laugh, son, but it's true," he asserted in the good-natured, yet serious, way he had.

"Do you mean to tell me that you're going to be killed on this corner?" I asked.

"That's right," he answered soberly.

When the lights changed, we crossed the street. I said to Sam, "If you know that you're going to be killed here, why do you take this way home? You could walk a block east or west and take the streetcar from there."

"It wouldn't be much use trying to avoid it," he answered. "Some day I'd forget, or have some business to transact down here—"

"Well, suppose you decided not to die at all. You could move to another town and live forever."

"Nobody lives forever," he answered patiently. "You can't avoid your fate. This is where it will happen, and nothing I can do will prevent it. I'm just hoping that it won't be for some time yet." He looked up at me and smiled apologetically, but I could see that he meant every word.

After that I brought the subject up occasionally as we were crossing Adelaide street, kidding him about being short-sighted, and about getting killed before his time if he wasn't careful. He would only smile at me and say, "You wait and see."

Last night we left the office as usual, about two minutes to five, in order to beat the rush to the elevators. Sam bought his paper in the lobby, and we went out into the street.

As we brushed through the five-o'clock crowd I asked Sam how his dike drawings for the Mountainview Refinery were coming along, and he told me he expected to finish them in a week; he was only waiting for some new tank specifications from McGuire, one of the engineers.

Looking up into the blue sky above the buildings I said, "It's going to be a nice evening. A change from the rain we've been having."

"Yes, it is. I'm going to do a little lawn bowling tonight," he answered. "It'll be my first chance this year. The greens have been a mess up to now."

When we reached the corner of Adelaide the lights were in our favour and we began to cross with the crowd. They changed from green to amber when we were half-way across, but we still had plenty of time. He stuck close to me as he always did. I saw this taxi cut around the traffic and begin to cross the intersection as soon as it got the green light, so I shouted to Sam and ran the last few metres to the sidewalk.

I looked around and saw the taxi pick him up and throw him with a sickening plop against a hydrant about six metres from the corner. There was the scream of the taxi's brakes and a lot of yelling from the crowd.

By the time I got there two men had laid Sam out on the sidewalk. Everybody was crowding around to get a better look at him. He was dead, of course. One side of his head was squashed like the soft spot in an orange.

A policeman butted his way through the crowd and asked what had happened. The hack driver came over from his car and told the policeman that he hadn't had a chance, this old man ran right in front of his cab. He seemed to be a nice young fellow, and he wanted us all to believe him. I told the policeman I was a friend of Sam's, and that I'd seen the accident. I assured the driver that it wasn't his fault.

The taxi company lawyer came to my place later in the evening and questioned me about the accident. "I can't understand why he'd turn around and run the other way," he kept on saying.

"I've told you it wasn't your driver's fault, so why do you keep asking me questions like that?"

"O.K. I'm only trying to dope this thing out in case they have an inquest," he said.

If they have an inquest, I'm going to tell the truth. I've been thinking it over and I feel sure that Sam would have wanted it that way.

I had nothing against the old fellow, but after listening for so long to him, bragging about knowing where he was going to die, it seemed I had to find out whether he was right or not. When I shouted at him to turn back, it wasn't me talking at all. Call it fate or predestination, or what you like, but that's what killed Sam Glover.

226

LITTLE PARADISE

Z e n a   C o l l i e r

There was no longer any doubt about it; they were lost. This was their first time on the creek from which this maze of narrow waterways derived, winding around in convoluted curves, dotted at frequent intervals with tiny uninhabited islands, all of which looked alike. A friend had recommended the area. "Great for canoeing. Pleasing prospects at every turn. None of those damn speedboats and water-skiers." For the past hour, in fact, they had seen no other boats at all: no canoes or dinghies, no cabin cruisers with their seemingly mandatory quota of bluff types wearing commodore hats, holding martini glasses or beer. (Earlier that day, one such, at sight of their canoe, had leaned over the rail, hollering at them flapping a hand back and forth against his mouth to produce what was meant to be a war whoop. "Hey, you Tarzan, she Jane, huh?" Laughter.)

"What time is it getting to be?" Peter asked.

"Just gone five." Frances rested her paddle for a moment.

They had been out since ten. All day the sun had shone from a cloudless sky, dappling the leaves of the branches that dipped over the water, stippling the water with shade. Insects with gossamer wings hummed past. Occasionally the *ts, ts, ts* of a cedar waxwing, the dry rattle of a kingfisher, broke the silence. Otherwise all was still.

It was the kind of day on which they congratulated themselves on their acquisition of the canoe. For people of their taste
and principles, the canoe had proved an ideal choice. It offered no
disturbance, by noise or pollution, to its passengers or to nature;
it required no particular skill, maintenance, or expensive berth-
ing. Best of all, it made easily possible days of escape from the
tensions of their everyday lives. Peter, a thin dark man with a face
all angles, was a graphics designer who had recently left his
agency job to free-lance. Frances, redhaired, with a pleasant
down-to-earth manner, was a social worker attached to one of
the great metropolitan hospitals. For both of them, a Saturday
spent this way brought a necessary renewal of the spirit.

It was with regret that they'd decided at four o'clock to start
for home. They were due at a party at seven; it was going to take
them a while to paddle back to the point of starting, then the drive
home would take the better part of an hour. So they had turned
around and headed back, stroking steadily. Until they'd become
aware, suddenly, that they had passed the same spot twice; they
recognized it because of an uprooted tree which lay in the water,
its exposed roots forming a natural driftwood sculpture upon
which someone had tossed, or placed, a beer can. ("Look at that,"
Frances had said earlier, shaking her head. The trappings of *their*
midday meal—paper plates, napkins, the bottle emptied of wine—
had been carefully stowed in a paper bag and replaced in the
canoe, to be properly disposed of on their arrival home.)

"We must have gone in a circle," Frances said.

"Keep going left. We'll hit the creek further on."

They resumed paddling.

"Are you tired?" Peter asked, after a while.

"No." In fact, she had begun to ache between the shoulder-
blades, but she knew that if she said so, Peter would suggest
putting on the motor and she didn't want that.

When he had first bought the motor, she had been very
much against it. An outboard on a canoe was surely a contradic-
tion? But there was a point to it, Peter maintained. "We'll use it
just to reach the outskirts of more remote areas, then take it off."
Still, the sound of the engine starting up always jarred her

unpleasantly, and ruined, she felt, the peace; she disapproved, too, of the trail of blue smoke it occasionally emitted, though Peter said that was just a matter of some needed adjustment.

"That island over there, with the willows, did we pass it before?"

"I don't know. They all look alike. Can't you tell from the sun?"

"I *thought* I could." He sounded exasperated.

"We're never going to make the Robsons' by seven."

Minutes later, the sound of the engine cut the still air, and they were moving along at a steady rate. But with little success. "We passed this before. I remember those sumacs..."

"Yes," Peter said wearily. "Now what?"

"Let's try over there." Frances pointed. "There was an inlet. Perhaps it leads somewhere."

The inlet narrowed after the first few metres, the banks growing gradually higher and closer. Soon the trees met overhead in a solid archway, the foliage forming a verdant tunnel as the passage between grew narrower and narrower.

Frances shivered. How dark it seemed, and cold.... Had the sun gone permanently, or was it just—

"We're coming out!"

Abruptly they were out of the dimness, out of the tunnel, finding themselves on a sunlit lake, a pond, really, perhaps a hundred metres across, with shallow sloping banks covered with woodland.

"Look!"

Across the pond was a house set almost at the water's edge, and beside it a redwood table where people sat, adults and children.

"Thank heaven! We can ask directions."

The people watched as the canoe put-putted across the pond toward them. In the still and sunlit scene, the motor sounded terribly loud. A desecration, Frances thought, regretting it, sorry not only to be invading these people's privacy but to be disturbing the peace of this serene spot.

But the adults—two women and two men—smiled at them

as the canoe approached. Peter idled the motor, then reached out and kept his hand on the bank, steadying the canoe as he talked.

"Sorry to disturb you, but we're lost. How do we get back to the start of Forked Creek?"

One of the men stood up and approached. "You're a long way off. It'll take you quite a while."

"Not with this." Peter nodded at the motor. But just then, as though on cue, the motor died. "Damn! Out of gas, I'm afraid. Can you by any chance let me have some fuel?"

"Sorry, we haven't any. We've no cars or powerboats or any such thing."

The others came over. The men admired the canoe and asked questions about the motor; they said they hadn't seen a motor on a canoe before. The children—a boy and girl in their early teens, and a little girl who seemed about five—stood watching and listening. The little girl said shyly, "I'm glad you're going to stay."

One of the women rumpled the child's blond curly hair. "This is my daughter Cassandra—Cassie."

Frances smiled at Cassie, an engaging child with sturdy, golden-brown baby-fat limbs. The whole group, in fact, was glowing with health, tanned by sun and wind; the women's dimpling smiles showed white even teeth; the men were tall, broad-shouldered, muscular, friendly.

"Would you care to join us for something to eat?" the other woman asked. "We're just starting dinner."

"Please do," Cassie's mother urged. "Just family style. I'm Amy Carner, by the way, and this is my husband Robert, and his brother Martin and Martin's wife Lorraine. And their twins, Andy and Jennifer."

"Do stay," Lorraine said. "Food'll give you energy for the return trip home. We'd love to have you."

"Yes, we would," Martin said.

Peter glanced at Frances. "We wouldn't want to impose—"

"No imposition at all," Robert said. "We don't get many visitors. Just, occasionally, people like yourselves, who end up here lost."

"Thtay, thtay," Cassie pleaded, finger in her mouth.

Frances's eyes met Peter's. The smell of meat cooking on the outdoor fireplace wafted over enticingly. They had eaten nothing at all for hours. And the Robsons were a lost cause by now.

"That's awfully kind of you. If you're sure—"

For answer, Robert bent down and pulled the canoe in to the bank. Martin put out a hand and helped Frances alight. Lorraine took them into the house to wash up.

Outside again, at the table, Frances realized just how hungry she was. She and Peter ate with enormous appetite. All the food was delicious: the salads and corn were homegrown; the steaks and hots were the best she'd ever tasted, Frances thought, and said so.

"This is a beautiful spot..." She glanced at the pond lying still as glass beneath the sun, at the greenness of the trees reflected in the water. No sign, besides themselves, of human habitation; nothing to spoil or disturb the scene's tranquility. "It must be lovely here in winter, too. Do you live here all year round?" she asked.

Amy nodded. It was like a Christmas card scene in winter, she said, when the pond froze and snow lay on the woods and the hills beyond.

"Though lately some rackety snowmobiles have come through." Martin sliced more meat and proffered the platter. "A couple of 'em came to a sticky end near here. Ever ridden one?"

"Not I." Peter took a bite of steak.

"Hate them," Frances said. "Fouling up the countryside."

Robert gave her a glance. "Yet you put on a motor—"

"That," Peter said, "was my idea. Fran was against it. But we only use it for certain contingencies."

"We've a rowboat, ourselves." Martin speared another sausage.

Lorraine passed potato salad.

"We do what we can, in our way, to preserve—"

"In our small way," Amy said. "Meat? Tomatoes, Peter? Frances?"

Not another thing, they protested, smiling, not another morsel of steak or succulent sausage, sun-warm tomato or butter-clad corn.

For dessert there was cherry pie with iced tea.

"Delicious." Peter slowly sipped the cool amber liquid. "Different."

Yes, it was an herbal tea, Amy said, her own recipe.

Frances drank hers slowly, leaving half—she'd never liked any kind of tea.

The sun lay low on the horizon now. Frances and Peter helped carry things into the house.

Andy and Jennifer appeared with fishing rods. "Where's the boat?"

"Being caulked," Robert said. "You can't take it."

"Oh." Andy turned to Peter. "Would it be O.K. if we use your canoe? They bite better out in the middle of the pond."

Peter hesitated. "We have to be getting along pretty soon."

Very soon, Frances thought; the canoe had no light, and being out on the water at night was not an inviting prospect.

"Is twenty minutes any good to you?"

"Great," Andy said. "Thanks a lot."

Cassie slipped her hand into Frances's. "Come and play with me."

"What shall we play?"

"I'll show you."

Cassie led her outdoors, round to the other side of the house. On a small patch of flagstone, she demonstrated a game played with coins, using the coins as play objects—a kind of Pitch Penny. She had a large stock of coins, of all denominations, kept in what was obviously an old purse of her mother's.

Once, as they played, a quarter pitched clumsily by Frances ended up in the grass. They searched but to no avail. "I'm sorry, Cassie."

"It doesn't matter. It's only game money."

"But—"

"I'll get more," Cassie said. "There's more when I want it. Daddy gives it to me."

They played several games. By now the house glimmered palely through the dusk; the shadows of evening were thickening everywhere.

Frances straightened. "That's it, Cassie. I have to go home now."

Cassie did not argue, just stood silent, finger in her mouth, as Frances turned and went in search of Peter.

She found him on the bank, with the others, looking out over the water. "Peter, shouldn't we—"

"Yes, we have to be getting along." He turned to the others. "We're very grateful for all your hospitality."

"You've been so kind," Frances said. "That marvelous dinner...this idyllic setting. Thank you for letting us share your little paradise."

"Must you rush off?"

"How about a drink? One for the road, as it were?"

They really had to get going, Peter said. "But thank you again, for everything."

Martin cupped his hands around his mouth. "Andy! Jennifer!" His voice rang across the dark mass of water. "Come along! Our guests are leaving!"

By now the youngsters were almost completely invisible. Andy's voice, floating back, seemed disembodied. "Just a minute—something's biting!"

Frances glanced at Peter, who shrugged. Clearly they would have to wait; they could hardly spoil the children's fun after accepting their parents' gracious hospitality.

"You see, you'll just have to come in for a nightcap." Martin's hand descended on Peter's shoulder.

They sat around the living room, sipping a liqueur that Robert had poured. Not the sort of thing Frances liked usually—and Peter, she knew, didn't care for it at all—an elderberry wine, or something like that, that Robert had made.

It must be the wine, combined with the rigours of the day, that was making her feel so sleepy now, she thought; it took a huge effort to keep her eyelids open. Seconds, later, in fact, she saw with dismay that Peter, slumped on the sofa flanked by

Robert and Martin, had yielded; his eyes were closed, his head tilted forward.

Dreadful! She began to stammer some kind of apology for their drowsiness. But where, oh where, were Andy and Jennifer? How could they go on fishing in the darkness like that, especially when they knew the canoe was needed?

As though the thought had given birth to the event, they appeared, carrying fishing gear. She tried to stand, to speak, but her legs were suddenly weak, her vision blurred, her thoughts addled.

Now her head sank irresistibly forward. But though her eyes closed she was not quite asleep, for she heard voices. Or was she in fact asleep and dreaming; were the voices part of the dream?

Not the woman. It wasn't her idea. That was Lorraine.

She's in it just as deeply as him.

Only a canoe...

But the motor... That was Robert.

On and on it went, a kind of debate. Parts of it she missed, as consciousness seemed to ebb and flow, the line lost between dream and reality.

Look. That was Andy. *We found these.*

Silence.

You see? Lorraine again. *They could have tossed that bottle, that trash, overboard. I vote we let them go. Anyway—*Someone walked across the room, drowning out the voice—*hardly worth it...not particularly large...*

Large...The canoe? "Let them go?"

Fear began at the edge of awareness, working inward like a worm in an apple.

Hush, she's stirring!

Someone approached, touched her, spoke her name. She let her head slump further forward.

Not she. They're out, both of them.

I want the money. That was Cassie, whining. *She lost one of my quarters.*

Goodness, child, you ought to be in bed! Amy, take her upstairs, it's long past her bedtime.

234

Be a good girl, Cassie, someone else said. *You'll get the money. You always do, don't you?*

Thieves, then? Common robbers, lying in wait for unwary boaters? But—

Complimented me on the way I cooked the steaks...

Laughter.

That was funny? The steaks?

A memory: the sight of the meat invitingly singed by the fire. The sausages. "We make them, ourselves," Amy had said.

Her thoughts spun like a Catherine wheel. Her heart pounded harder and harder—surely it would burst the flesh that housed it. Flesh.

Oh, God, she must be sick to be thinking this way, as sick as the rest of them, every one of them, the whole picturebook family with the bloom of health, the radiance of summer, upon them. Summer...And what of winter, the hapless snowmobile riders? Thought stopped at the unthinkable, ran screaming in the other direction. A dream, yes, a nightmare. Any moment now she would awake to see sunlight coming in the bedroom window, would get up, start breakfast, make plans with Peter for their day on the water.

All right. We've talked long enough. Robert cleared his throat.

No denying that sound—the reality of it. The reality of their situation, hers and Peter's here and now. Oh God, Peter, wake up! Though what could they do, even then, the two of them, trapped here? A diversion? What could take their attention, if only for a moment? But they would need, she and Peter, more than a moment to reach the canoe, then get away, paddling, across the water. Unless they left the canoe and tried through the woods. But—

A door slammed. A voice said excitedly, "Dad! Andy! Everybody, come out here!" The girl, Jennifer.

There was a rush of movement, footsteps, the door slammed again, then silence.

A hiss: "Fran!"

She opened her eyes, to meet Peter's. The room was empty except for themselves.

"Did you hear—?"

"Yes! What shall we do?"

"They're coming back! Play dead!"

The door opened again. There were hurrying footsteps, whispers. Robert's voice said, "Shake them, get them up! Hurry!"

A hand on her shoulder shook her, hard.

"Wake up, Frances! Peter! Time to go home. It's getting late." The tone was friendly, just the least bit urgent. "Sleepy? You'll be all right once you're outside."

What was this? For now, dazed, they were being led outside, urged along, hastened down to the canoe in the moonless night. Thick darkness..."You'll want to hurry...It's getting late. The long day must have been too much for you...sleeping like babies...."

Was that all it really was, after all? They had fallen asleep after the meal; it had all been a product of too much food and drink and fatigue?

They were in the canoe now, in the water, helped in by Martin and Lorraine. The canoe rocked. Robert steadied it carefully, placed paddles in their trembling hands. "Owe you an apology...motor's gone, I'm afraid. Andy and Jenny were fooling around...sank like a stone."

"Never mind!" Peter's voice was almost a croak. "Doesn't matter!"

They were off, paddling like demons, shivering, shivering in the sharp night air.

"To the left..." Martin's voice floated after them. "After you're through Scylla and Charybdis, go right three times, then left at the uprooted tree. You'll see it."

They would, for now a moon emerged from the clouds, painting the scene with a frozen light.

"What happened?" Frances whispered.

"God knows! Keep going!"

The canoe cut swiftly across the water. But as the darkness of the tunnel yawned before them, Frances hesitated, turned, and saw a cabin cruiser pulling close to shore, several figures on deck.

A voice floated across the water. "…don't know how we could have missed our way like that…"

"We must warn them, Peter! We have to warn them!"

He pushed her around. "Keep going. There's nothing we can do."

In the blackness of the tunnel, the only sound was the soft *slap* of the paddles dipping in the water, while from somewhere far away came the high, screeching giggle of a loon.

ACKNOWLEDGEMENTS

The publishers have made every effort to trace the source of materials appearing in this book. Information that will enable the publishers to rectify any error or omission will be welcomed.

"Rick Hansen: Man in Motion" by Richard Scrimger. Reprinted by permission of the author.

"Raymond's Run" copyright © 1970 by Toni Cade Bambara. Reprinted from GORILLA, MY LOVE by Toni Cade Bambara, by permission of Random House, Inc.

"The Greatest Victory" by Frank O'Rourke. Reprinted by permission of Carlson & Nichols, agents for the author's estate.

"The Most Important Day" from THE STORY OF MY LIFE by Helen Keller. Published by Doubleday, a division of Bantam, Doubleday, Dell Publishing Group, Inc. Reprinted by permission of the publisher.

"The Breakthrough" excerpted from JONATHAN LIVINGSTON SEAGULL by Richard Bach. Reprinted with permission of Macmillan Publishing Company. Copyright © 1970 by Richard Bach and Leslie Parrish-Bach.

"Why Was Elena Crying?" copyright © 1982 by Norma Fox Mazer. Reprinted by permission of the author.

"Young and In Love With Their Wheels" by June Callwood. Reprinted by permission of the author.

"A Good Time Tonight" excerpted and adapted from A GOOD TIME TONIGHT by Gary and Louise Hodge. Reprinted by permission of Thomas Nelson Australia. [Note: The story reprinted here is one of six centred around the death of teenager, Mandy Sokolich, as she is travelling home from an end-of-term party. The stories are told from six points of view: that of Helga, a close friend; Bev, Mandy's mother; Mario, an acquaintance of Mandy; Mandy's boyfriend, Simon; Danny, a close friend of Simon and Mandy; and Brad, a young police officer on his first fatal accident assignment. The six stories interrelate so that a picture of Mandy is built up through the way she enters the various characters' lives.]

"Sally" from the book THOSE AMAZING ⏐ELECTRONIC MACHINES: AN ANTHOLOGY OF ROBOT AND COMPUTER STORIES by Isaac Asimov. Reprinted with permission of the publisher, Franklin Watts.

"Be It Ever So Rent Free" from FATHERHOOD, by Bill Cosby. Copyright © 1986 by William H. Cosby, Jr. Reprinted by permission of Doubleday, a division of Bantam, Doubleday, Dell Publishing Group, Inc.

PHOTOGRAPHS

ILLUSTRATIONS